D1523852

Mirrors
&
Windows

Reflections on the Journey

in Serious Illness Practice

Mirrors & Windows

ACKNOWLEDGMENTS

We would like to thank all the contributors to this book. Their names, credentials and area of practice can be found in the next pages. You have shared your perspectives so graciously, with honesty and care. Please know that we are deeply grateful that you have brought us into your worlds.

Cover photograph is courtesy of Faye Cornish on Unsplash.com

DISCLAIMER

Names of patients, family members, colleagues have been changed to protect the identities of those individuals.

SANKOFA

Depicted by the Adinkra symbols of a mythical bird
and stylized heart Sankofa stems from the Twi
language of the Akan people of Ghana and invites us
to:

San "return"; ko "go" and fa "look, seek & take."

CONTRIBUTORS

Katie Aliberti, MA, MSW, LCSW
Mental Health Clinician

Terry Altilio, LCSW, APHSW-C
Palliative Social Work

Esther Ammon, LCSW, APHSW-C
Pediatric Palliative Care

Autumn Asher BlackDeer, PhD, MSW
Consultation

Christine Beamon, LCSW, CCM, APHSW-C
Palliative Medicine Social Worker

Tracy Borgmeyer, MSW, MA, LCSW, HEC-C
Medical Ethics Consultation

Stephanie Broadnax Broussard, LCSW-S, APHSW-C
Oncology Palliative Care, Counseling

Chelsea Brown, LCSW, APHSW-C, CCTP
Inpatient Palliative Care

Jennifer Hill Buehrer, LMSW, HEC-C
Inpatient Palliative Care Consultation

Rebecca Cammy, MSW, LCSW
Oncology, Palliative Care

Sharon Chung, LICSW, APHSW-C
Therapist: Serious illness, grief and loss

Nancy Cincotta, LCSW, MPhil, CPA (Narrative Medicine)
Pediatric Oncology, Pediatric Palliative Care, end of life,
bereavement

Susan Conceicao, LCSW, AHPSW-C
Teaching and Clinical Supervision; Private Psychotherapy
Practice

Halee Dams, MSW, LICSW
Palliative Care & Bereavement Counselor

Louisa Daratsos, PhD, LCSW
Inpatient and Outpatient Oncology & Palliative Care

Jill Farabelli, LCSW, APHSW-C
Inpatient/Outpatient Palliative Care

Anne Front, MA, LMFT, APHSW-C
Palliative Care

Adie Goldberg, DSW, LICSW
Inpatient and Palliative Care Consultation

Susan Hedlund, LCSW, FAOSW
Oncology Social Work

Philip Higgins, PhD, LICSW
Psychotherapy and Palliative Care Consultation

Anne Kelemen, LICSW, APHSW-C
Inpatient Palliative Care

Charisse Knowlan, MSW, RSW
Palliative Care Social Worker

Nina Laing, LICSW, APHSW-C
Inpatient Palliative Care Consultation

Abigail Latimer, PhD, MSW, LCSW, APHSW-C
Outpatient Palliative Care; Palliative Care Research

Lauren LaTourette, LCSW, APHSW-C
Inpatient Palliative Care

Eunju Lee, LCSW, APHSW-C, MSOD
Oncology, Palliative, and End-Of-Life Care

Vickie Leff, LCSW, APHSW-C
Education, Palliative Care Consultation

Jennifer Christophel Lichti, MSW, LICSW, BCD,
APHSW-C
Outpatient Palliative Care

Michael A. Light, MSW, MPH, LICSW, LMP, APHSW-C
Homeless Outreach Palliative Care; Education & Research

Meagan Lyon Leimena, MSW, MPH
Palliative Social Work Consultant

Sheri Mila Gerson, PhD, LICSW, APHSW-C
Private Counseling and Consultation Practice

Ta'Tiana Miles, LGSW
Inpatient Palliative Care Consultation

Abigail Nathanson, LCSW, DSW, APHSW-C, ACS
Outpatient Mental Health; Trauma, loss and illness

Arden O'Donnell, MPH, MSW, LICSW, APHSW-C
Inpatient Palliative Care

Carina Oltmann, MSSW, LCSW
Inpatient Palliative Care

Chris Onderdonk, MSW, LCSW, APHSW-C
Inpatient Palliative Care

Shirley Otis-Green, MSW, MA, ACSW, LCSW, OSW-CE,
FNAP, FAOSW
Palliative Care Consultant

Arika Moore Patneaude, MSW, LICSW, APHSW-C
Pediatric Palliative Care, Ethics, Anti-racism Consultant

Nicholas Purol, MSW, LICSW
Pediatric Palliative Care

Maxxine Rattner, MSW, RSW
Hospice/Palliative Care Clinician Educator

Stacy S. Remke, LICSW. APHSW-C
Pediatric Palliative Care

Dana Ribeiro Miller, M.Div., LCSW, APHSW-C
Inpatient Palliative Care/Clinical Instructor of Medicine

Rachel Rusch, LCSW, MSW, MA, APHSW-C
Pediatric Palliative Care – Education, research & practice

S. "Eryl" Shermak, BA, MSW, PhD, RSW
Community Health Services

Allie Shukraft, MSW, MAT, APHSW-C
Pediatric Palliative Care

Bridget Sumser, LCSW
Palliaitve Care Education

Laurel Tropeano, LCSW, APHSW-C
Palliative Care Consultation; Social Work Education

Clara Van Gerven, APHSW-C
Inpatient Hospice

Cara Wallace, PhD, LMSW, APHSW-C
Researcher and Educator; former Hospice Social Worker

INTRODUCTION

Caring for our fellow humans with serious illness can be intense, gratifying, and challenging, clinically, operationally and emotionally. Some refer to it as a "calling", others fell into it and discovered that they could manage the multitude of emotions that often exist. The joy and heartache that can come with navigating relationships with one's patients, their caregivers, and their communities pulls those of us in serious illness care in a multitude of directions. Add to this what it means to be a good clinician, a good team member, a good advocate all while navigating systems of hierarchy, oppression, structural racism, and limited resources.

Our intention with this book is to create a space for us to pause, to reflect, to be in community. To give space to the very human interactions that stay with us, the ones that keep us up at night, that push us, challenge us and at times change who we are as clinicians and human beings. To express gratitude for lessons received, to mourn lives lost, to acknowledge where we may have been complicit, to see each other and those we show up to support through the door of humanity. All without judgement.

In healthcare, this space is too often consumed by the rush to do the next thing, to save the next life, to have the next conversation, to focus on productivity and the bottom line.

This book is meant as a repository for those of us who work in palliative care, in hospice, in serious illness to place the emotions, the learnings, the reflections. It is a space for us to hold up a mirror and see ourselves for who we are, the good, the bad and the ugly, and consider how we contribute, to not just the field of serious illness care, but to each other as humans. This book is also a window for us to gaze through, to open up, to breathe through. It is a connector of the personhood that we each have and share with those we care for and with our interprofessional colleagues. Growth happens when we can look inward, pause, and reflect, on what went well, what did not and what at times goes horribly wrong. It is through acknowledging the humanity in ourselves that we touch and reflect back the humanity in others. We invite you to join us on this journey.

Terry Altilio
Anne Kelemen
Vickie Leff
Arika Moore Patneaude

Mirrors

Photo by <u>Zeynep Sümer</u> on <u>Unsplash</u>

Katie Aliberti

How We Remember

Given some of my experiences, looking back, it seems inevitable that I would find myself working with individuals at the end of their lives. My mother has been a nurse for my whole life but in the mid-eighties to early-nineties, she worked at a maximum security prison almost exclusively with individuals with HIV and AIDS. It was a scary time in healthcare, and she was sometimes the only staff nurse willing to provide care. She was always transparent about her work and would come home telling us stories of her patients. Her world became our world too. We knew her patients, their stories, and their deaths. They felt forgotten and sometimes she was the only one who could remember them after they died, the only person who could tell their stories. Their families and friends were often long gone. I remembered thinking how important it was that someone remembered them. In grade school, my mother set me up with my first pen pal, who was on death row. I became aware of how close he stood to death and what it might feel like for him to live in that space.

I was drawn to palliative care with the understanding and

the belief that there are as many stories as there are people. One of the roles I have had as a palliative care social worker is to be a vessel for others. Sometimes we hold their truths, their dreams, their sadness, or their hopes. In the decade plus that I spent in palliative care and hospice, I have held onto pieces of so many of my patients over the years. I have always felt that I bring little bits of them with me wherever I go and sometimes I share them with others so that the stories go on. I remember pieces of their lives, or people who were important to them, their work, or some bit of advice they passed along.

It was nearly five o'clock in the morning on a Tuesday when I received a text message from my brother telling me that my sister was in the intensive care unit. A relatively healthy forty-nine-year-old, my initial thoughts were hopeful. Subsequent conversations with hospital staff revealed what had happened. She had been experiencing abdominal pain throughout the day but refused to go to the doctor. Like many others, she had no insurance and was still paying a previous hospital bill from another illness years before. At some point, she collapsed and stopped breathing. She was resuscitated a total of six times between her home and the hospital. By the time we saw her in the hospital, she was on six pressors, intubated, and on a ventilator. After so many family meetings, I was sitting on the other side of the table. It was both easier and harder than I thought it would be. I knew everything they were telling me, and I knew what it meant. I was able to clinically distance myself and make decisions.

Uninsured with a toxicology screen positive for drugs, it felt like she "was one of the forgotten ones." The challenge was the knowledge that everything could have been done better, done differently instead of leaving us with the feeling that "she just didn't matter." They asked nothing about her and learned little. There was no social worker or palliative care team, so we were left alone to navigate this space. For others with less experience, it would have been daunting. Death, of course, is an inevitability for all of us. We will all experience loss and circumnavigate the dark waters associated with grief. Every single one of us has a story (or stories) to tell. We all deserve to have someone who can recall and remember some bit about us that is meaningful.

Terry Altilio

I Often Wonder How I Got Here...

I am the only and middle daughter in an Italian second-generation family. I was taught to sew by age eleven and the following Christmas, I received a gift box of a silver spoon. Why would anyone get a silver spoon for Christmas? The cultural messaging was soon dwarfed by the death from cancer of the matriarch in this family - a death that launched a cacophony of consequential events - remarriage, alcohol abuse, job loss, incarceration, a brother's death by suicide and more. While I went from sewing and silver spoons to an expectation for college, the fatherly advice was "learn how to type so you can always be a secretary." I smile as I type this reflection with two and sometimes three fingers.

I often think it has been serendipity that shaped future chapters of this story; countered the sadness, the potential for numbing. While privilege got me to graduate school and gave me years to be a full-time parent and dabble in local politics, dependency again became untenable when another job loss propelled me toward full-time work. It seems serendipitous that a local hospital hired this social worker

4

with no healthcare experience to join an oncology unit. Serendipitous that learning was accessible and supervision gracious and supportive and that future positions became platforms to learn, write and teach. There were no boundaries really around work and home nor around the revelations, the whispered thoughts and feelings that occupied my mind and heart and linked personal history to patients, families—the struggles with team members; the silence I might have chosen when my voice needed to be heard. Tears and anger came less often as validation from colleagues became less important and I stopped waiting for others to tell me *what my job was*. Respectful disagreement deepened understanding, replacing judgment of others with a fledgling compassion that we need for self and each other. Serendipity came to be enriched by reflective and intimate moments with patients, their families and colleagues bringing an opportunity to touch lives and stand in awe of the mystery and magic in unique yet shared aspects of their stories. It might have begun with Jonathon the young actor with recurrent testicular cancer who was filled with dread and pain so haunting that he considered suicide. Years later I would run into his mother in a deli. She said, "I know you; you saved my life—you took care of Jonathon."

This mom taught me the comforting and challenging truth—that serendipity can bring us in touch with the unspoken ways we impact lives into the future. Perhaps it was the sisters, Maria, age six, and Sophia, age eight, who sat in the waiting room of the intensive care unit because their father felt it would do harm if they were to see their mother. Maria declared—"she is our mother; he has no right to say we cannot see her."

As I helped their father re-imagine a future should his daughters not be able to visit their mom, her nurse created a scene of comfort and caring, and Maria and Sophia were prepared to visit. Perhaps it was Maria who would later compose a letter to read to her seemingly unresponsive mother. Or the adolescent with Duchenne muscular dystrophy who could engage his eighteen-year-old mind to conjure an image of his five-year-old body floating up and out of the intensive care unit or the young mother, with bones breaking from metastatic disease, who imagined her path "to the mountaintop" in her home country of Trinidad. Or the daughters who asked that we hasten their mom's death because "she never wanted to wait in line." or our outpatient who calmly described a family reunion in Georgia.

"I do not like to go there; there are opossums, it is too quiet and there are trees where people were lynched."

There may always be a touch of mystery as to how one's life evolves. Amidst this mystery I have been blessed to share treasured memories, join in moments, hushed and clamorous, that lit the path toward a modicum of healing, a mitigation of judgment—engaged much joy along with shared sorrows.

Autumn Asher BlackDeer

The Mission of Social Work

I came to social work from the battle trenches of inpatient psychiatric facilities, working with adolescents with behavioral disorders in the residential program. I sat with them as they wrote letters, colored pictures, and completed activities all to show their parents what progress they were making. I held their hands as they realized the real challenge began once they return home to contend with their living situation, school stress, and overall tension in the household. While most regarded the teenagers as a lost cause, even referring to their unit as the wolf den, I refused to heed warnings of "dangerous" clients, typically those of color, and dared to treat them as equals. I was just a behavioral health tech at the time, but the director of clinical services (Licensed Clinical Social Worker) encouraged me to pursue social work in order to be able to make greater change and have more influence over patient care.

Once in my MSW program, I was quickly disheartened with the actuality of the profession. So many courses focused solely on monitoring and reporting, adjusting to the status quo, and teaching our clients how to do the same. Where was the opportunity to influence patient care? How is self-determination ever actualized in clinical practice? Are the values and ethics merely lip service? Even in my practicum experiences, field instructors lamented how certain clients unfairly distrust white social workers, supervisors again warning me to watch out for my safety around Black and Brown clients, the microaggressions abound. From the classroom to the field, social work was increasingly disappointing and ultimately unacceptable.

Then came Cindy Howard, practicum supervisor, and one of the longest standing social work legacies in the state of Oklahoma. She supervised our practicum site rotations, remaining our constant liaison despite the changing agencies and organizations within which we learned. She held monthly seminars for us to bring our practicum experiences and process what we had observed, giving us the opportunity to bridge the classroom content with the actuality of the field. Throughout the year she imparted wisdom from her decades of experience and challenged us to practice and implement what social work truly is. One of her most famous sayings that continues to guide my practice to this day is, "Social work is not a job; it's a mission."

True social work practice is a mission. It's not merely a profession of workers, marching forth and following orders.

Embodied social work actively centers social justice, works towards achieving the mission at hand, and is unafraid to do the necessary work to achieve true change. The great social problems of our time, the ongoing injustices our clients contend with, require fierce advocacy. Our clients can't wait for systems change, and we can't afford to continue perpetuating the status quo. Social work is indeed a mission, but will we rise to the occasion?

Rebecca Cammy

Too Close to Home

Repeatedly bearing witness to human suffering is emotionally taxing. And when the work hits too close to home, it can be almost unbearable. My friend was diagnosed with stage four rectal cancer in January 2018. She received treatment at the same cancer center where I have worked for over four years and was closely followed by my palliative care team.

I tried to maintain my distance in my friend's decision-making and optimistic spirit while remaining present and meeting her wherever she was in that moment in her cancer journey. I felt burdened by the knowledge from my professional role. I was internally conflicted—I wanted to be there for my friend but also needed to be realistic.

I toed the line of friend and healthcare professional daily. As her disease progressed, I was a bystander to team conversations about her care behind closed doors. I knew too much. It often seemed surreal. As my friend started to look sicker, I tried to pull myself together in the infusion suite while staying connected with my feelings. I felt trapped—I didn't know my role, like I couldn't be a friend

11

or a professional.

My friend died from her cancer this past spring. Three months before her death, I had the opportunity to process my emotions with Jenny Hegland, a listener poet through the Good Listening Project. For twenty minutes, she listened as I contemplated the heartache and tragedy I was experiencing. And through my friends', and subsequently my suffering, Jenny gave me the gift of poetry:

Her time is likely
Short

I dip one toe
Into the emotion
Fear, trepidation, tragedy

Hearts torn open
Trapped behind walls
Made of dreams
Still deserving their day

This landslide
Could sweep away
Cinder block homes

So I turn back, grasp
Practical, rational
Responsibility

determination and autonomy when the rest of the team disagrees. This is where our work as palliative social workers shines the brightest. I share with my patients that your goals are our goals as long as informed consent is met in conversation about their illness and decisions made. Wade was highly informed and politely disagreed.

Halee Dams

The First Time I Was Fired

I was a (relatively) young hospice social worker, and I was buzzing with energy and excitement for my career. We sat in an interdisciplinary team meeting (IDT) discussing a patient and family that staff were having difficulty engaging. My supervisor let me know she had been fired by the family and wondered if I could take over as their social worker. My immediate secret thought was that I could win them over. *I know she's really good, but I'm going to charm their socks off. I'm going to learn from her mistakes, and they're going to love me. There must've been something she missed, something she didn't do quite right.* I would be the social worker to crack the code.

I met the family, and of course it was a complex situation. A man in his fifties, dying of cancer, with a history of substance use and abuse within the home. Realizing he was about to die; he flew across the country to live with his daughter so she could take care of him. His estranged wife followed him to help, because it felt like the right thing for her to do. Many years of trauma and abuse and sadness and hurt, essentially put on the back burner while dad does the hard work of dying. I should've seen all the warning signs. The burnout from the family. Feeling like they had to walk on eggshells for fear of setting him off. His worsening anger and confusion and vulnerability as his health declined. I had clinical skills and abilities to support folks through difficulties such as these, didn't I?

I can say fairly that I did my best. You know those cases where you feel like you're working ten times harder than the family, and one patient is taking up more energy than the rest of your caseload combined? Unfortunately, despite my best efforts, I could not fix this incredibly difficult, complex, and heartbreaking situation. Of course, I couldn't! I could not find immediate, permanent placement for this man who was uninsured and dying. And in the end, I too was inevitably fired by the family. They screamed at me. Did not want me on the property! Never wanted to see my face again!

I sat in my car and cried and called my mom. It really hurt because I really cared and really tried! I felt like a failure as a social worker, personally attacked, and angry that this family couldn't see how much I wanted to help. With all this distance now, of course the situation unfolded exactly as it did. The family had so much anger, and nowhere to put it. My role there played out exactly as it was meant to. I can only hope that throughout the process perhaps I provided some comfort, or some peace. This wasn't the first time I was taught this lesson and am sure it won't be the last. How many times was I yelled at in the intensive care unit as a palliative social worker? Sometimes (a lot of the time) it's easier to be mad at the social worker than it is to be mad at God, or your dying father. Sometimes that is our role to play, and we can carry that hurt and anger for a family so they can live through their worst day a little bit lighter.

It's good to remember humility. Why did I think I knew better than my supervisor? In our next IDT meeting, I shared that I too had been fired, and needed another social worker to take over.

"Difficult families love me! I'll take it on " was the quick response from another young colleague of mine.

Some lessons will be taught over and over in this field, and each time we'll learn a bit more from them. If I can remain a student, I'll consider that a success. (And sometimes I'll need to call my mom crying and that's okay too.)

Louisa Daratsos

Did My Profession Find Me or Did I Find My Profession?

I love to ask that question of others at work. I can say I was born to do what I do. At five months old, my father's two youngest brothers died in a boating accident. My father's other brother loaned them the boat. These boys, as the family still calls them, were the pride of our Greek family. They were eighteen and twenty-one, the only ones to go to college and they had aspirations to become a doctor and a lawyer respectively. My first memory is of my paternal grandfather's funeral when I was three; I remember seeing my father weep. Although people could imagine great sadness in our family, my grandmother's house was still the place where everyone gathered on Sunday and extended kin coming from Greece got their first job working for my father's company.

When I was about eleven, the patriarch of my mother's family, her Uncle Paul developed lung cancer. My mother's father died during the Great Depression leaving his wife, my grandmother, a young immigrant widow with three children

21

and no source of support. Uncle Paul put his life on hold and did everything he could to help raise my mother's family. When Uncle Paul got lung cancer in the 1960's my mother became the designated caregiver. She and I picked him up from his hospital in Poughkeepsie, New York where he lived and worked as a cook. We brought him home to my maternal grandmother's home and my mother commuted daily to care for him. She learned how to clean the scars from his operation and when he received radiation therapy at Memorial Sloan Kettering Cancer Center, she scheduled the treatments after school so I could go with them.

A few years after Uncle Paul died, my mother's sister developed breast cancer. She was younger than my mother and my cousins needed caregiving as well. My grandmother lived in the same house and had limited ways to process what was happening to the people in her life as she was aging. By now I was in college—I still knew nothing about social work, palliative care, death and dying but I appreciated that my family did not shield me from real life, and I learned early on that good and bad things happen.

Eventually, I found my way into the social work profession and medical social work seemed like the only fit for me. I was incredibly lucky to be hired by the Veterans Health Administration (VA) and to work in a VA hospital.

Finally getting the position as the Psychosocial Coordinator of Oncology/Palliative Care was my dream job. I will never know what it is like to be in anyone else's position, but I hope that my lived experience, my studies, and my compassion is enough to help my patients and loved ones.

Adie Goldberg

A Mouse, Moguls and an MSW

I love the childhood book *Frederick,* the story of a mouse who spent the summer on a rock in the sun while all the other mice collected seeds and nuts to store for the winter. All the mice chastised Frederick and asked him what he was doing to help prepare for winter. He continued to sit on the rock in the sun. When winter came, the mouse community ate the seeds and the nuts, but winter lingered, and the supply dwindled. It was then that Frederick's work on the rock saved the community. Frederick had been sitting in the sun collecting stories. He shared those stories, warming his mouse family with recollections of the sun and filling their stomachs with stories of the bounty of summer.

I love being a social worker. Like Frederick, our job is to collect stories. When sitting with others in distress, social workers reach for the story. Amidst COVID and the fallout of increasing exhaustion and decreasing workforce numbers, we are asked to do more with less and witness a different type of distress wherever we turn. There are so many stories to hold.

Sadly, as I listen to hospital staff, my old responses to painful stories sound hollow. During the first wave of COVID, we reminded ourselves and each other this is why we chose our profession. Now that we are facing the threat of new variants, flu, and cultural malaise, it is different. It has overwhelmed us in a myriad of ways. Webinars, free books, inspirational stories and podcasts, and on-call mental health professionals with drop-in hours are not doing it. The caregiving websites might have been easily navigated pre-COVID but are now perceived as overwhelming and difficult to operate.

I am a downhill skier and when I get into difficulty on a steep run, I'm not open to a lesson or advice, I just want to get down. I call it survival skiing. It may not be pretty but once at the lodge you can talk to me about how I might have done it differently. In the moment, I just want you to ski next to me and let me know I'm not alone.

When our ancient predecessors were being attacked by wooly mammoths, it was not a moment to assess options, second guess impressions or ruminate. Survival was based on instincts. When cortisol and adrenaline increase, ability to assimilate new information decreases.

COVID and its fallout are redefining our personal narratives but there is no time now to fully reflect on their meaning. I don't want to shame the nurse who was given a book on trauma stewardship but is too exhausted to open it. I don't want the program director to feel guilty that they have not reached out to the free mental health services in order to better assist staff.

I wonder how much individuals, barely able to show up for work, are berating themselves for not … reading the book, reaching out to the free mental health service, practicing mindfulness, or writing poetry. I'm learning I just need to ski next to you and let you know I see you and I see the struggle. It is the work version of survival skiing.

Yes! The work of a social worker is vital to the community (rodent, human or otherwise). We need to get through this and when we do, the social workers will be there like Frederick, listening to your stories as you grieve the loss of your pre-COVID self and making sense of this moment as we all move forward with new understanding. For now, however, the best this social worker can muster is profound gratitude.

Thank you all for showing up.

Susan Hedlund

About Annie

I t has been about twelve years since Annie died. Annie was my patient for ten years. She was my age. She was diagnosed with breast cancer at age thirty-seven, with a recurrence seven years later, and lived with metastatic disease for another ten years. I miss her to this day, I think of her often, it is safe to say: "I loved her".

I currently work in a large, academic medical center. In my role, I am often called upon to help departments who are dealing with staff stressors, unexpected change, and sometimes, loss.

Over the last month I have been asked to support staff in departments who are dealing with the recent deaths of young faculty members. Both died of cancer, both left toddlers behind. The grief in our sessions is palpable, the helplessness and pain are in the air of heaviness, silence, and sorrow.

In one such session I met with a group of nine fourth-year medical residents, all of whom happened to be women. Many said they came to our program because of the young woman who recently died. She had come up through the

27

ranks—as a resident, a chief resident, and ultimately a faculty member. In theory, she had "arrived". She married, had a baby, and was looked to as a mentor, a warrior of doing the "right things" for the most vulnerable of patients.

Then she got sick, then she died. These lovely young residents asked: "Why her?", "Why now?"

"Why not me?" And other existential questions around their life choices: "If I have postponed so many things in life to this end, and then one gets sick and dies, why am I doing this?"

Questions about priorities, life's choices, and the unanswerable questions of "why?" sat with heaviness in the room.

So how does this connect with Annie? Many of us who do this work in oncology and palliative care have patients who have changed us...for the better. Under other circumstances, Annie could have been my good friend. In groups and counseling sessions, she made it so very clear, how important it was to live life now. She challenged me, and all of her health care providers, to tell the truth—in kind ways—while not giving up on her.

When Annie chose to avail herself of Medical Aid in Dying, she challenged me (as well as her beloved oncologist) to walk with her through that journey. We did. She chose a date, and I met, one by one, with each of her beloved family members and friends, to attempt to provide support. Walking with her and being there during her transition was one of the most beautiful experiences I have known. It was death on her terms. It was peaceful, it was quick, and all of her family supported and surrounded her with love.

The most recent death of my young colleague held a stark contrast. She was determined to hold on, no doubt to stay alive for her young daughter, to preserve her own life, and all the potential that lay ahead. She rejected any suggestion of palliative care or hospice. She too died on her own terms. She too was surrounded by the love of her colleagues and family. These deaths change me. In my most hopeful moments, they teach me about what is important in life, as well as the reminder to show up each day with openness and curiosity with our patients. In my harder moments, I still return to the questions of "why?", although through most of these years of work, I have tried not to. So, at the end of all this, where will we arrive? My hope for those of us who do this work is that we will remain open and curious, and not succumb to bitterness, anger, or burnout.

As Mary Oliver asks of us, what is your hope for this one wild and precious life?

I hope we all continue to consider that question. At the end of the day—this day, and most, I am forever grateful and changed by the experience.

Thank you, Annie, and my young colleague, for reminding me of these lessons.

Phil Higgins

How I Learned to Take the Stairs

Angela Clemons was an elegant woman even on her deathbed. Tall and lissome, her smooth skin belied her eighty-one years. She was a nurse who, together with her schoolteacher husband, had been part of the Black middle-class diaspora to Co-Op City in the Bronx in the 1960s, hoping to give their two daughters a better chance.

Here those daughters sat now, one on either side of their mother's bed on the fourth floor of the cancer hospital where she'd been admitted three weeks ago with the certainty that this was also where she would die. They had sat vigil together for the better part of each day, leaving only for quick overnights at home and never on the same night.

I was a very green second-year intern, excited to be in the hospital after a first year mostly spent trying to melt into the walls while I supervised visits between children and their non-custodial parents. It was dull and uncomfortable work to me, and I'm certain my own disgruntlement robbed me of the importance it held.

But this! Working at this fabled institution was a dream

come true. Finally, I'd be able to put my nascent clinical skills to work after hour upon hour spent under buzzing fluorescent lights detailing the movements of those angry, embarrassed parents. Finally, I'd get to work with the dying and the bereaved and the soon-to-be bereaved.

When I was called into Mrs. Clemons' room, two months into my fall semester, I felt ready. She was my supervisor's patient and I'd met her only once. It was a brief visit and I'd mostly stayed on the sidelines, eager to observe and rendered sheepish in the presence of such regal, high cheek boned greatness. Angela's dark eyes had caught mine and from her silk-pillowed perch she'd winked at me. I'd smiled back, betrayed by my Irish roots as a red flush colored my cheeks.

Angela's daughters gazed up at me and smiled as I entered. They asked me to join them and a few others in prayer as their mother was ready to move on. I stood at the foot of Angela's bed, my eyes fixed on the two steep hills, her long toes formed under the sheets and joined hands. Words were spoken and I thanked my own God that nobody asked me to speak. Before we'd finished, Angela took her final breath and was gone. Just like that. Nobody cried, but the still quiet in the room pressed down on my chest. I stayed for a bit, doing my best to comfort even as I felt a familiar discomfort in my own throat.

My feet carried me out of the room as if on a moving sidewalk, directly to the nearest stairwell door. When the door closed behind me, I collapsed against the cool, painted cinder block wall, my vision flashing hotly as my body shook and I released a deep, echoing sob. *What was happening? Why was I so distraught? I'd hardly known this woman!* My mind raced to regain control. I was certain someone would walk by, and I'd be humiliated, revealed for the imposter I was. The tears continued to flow, my cries continuing to bounce down four flights of stairs and back up again.

What I learned the next day, when the tears had dried and I'd had time to process it all with my supervisor, was that my reaction was natural for a newcomer who hadn't yet learned to squeeze out the sponge after each loss, but who had instead soaked in death after death. I hadn't, it turned out, ever actually really processed these losses. And so that's what I learned to do. After each visit with a patient—final or otherwise—I'd take the stairs. They'd almost always be empty, and I'd walk them slowly, my footsteps echoing on each stair, fingertips trailing along the railing, and take a minute to process what had just happened, to make space for the sacredness as well as the surrealism of this work.

I've walked an awful lot of stairwells in twenty years.

33

Nina Laing

Marked

Whodden I set out to be a social worker, I did not know exactly what that meant, nor how the work would take shape in my life once I was one. Most of us are drawn to this work out of a desire to make change, to help, to correct for society's wrongs or support the efforts of others in improving their lives. In reflecting back over the last thirteen years, it is not my impact on the world but rather, its impact on me that is most tangible. Most of the people encountered in this work likely don't recall the interaction. Yet, I find myself carrying bits of their stories, parts of a life of so many people whose paths have crossed mine, however briefly, forever changing me in some small way.

I am marked by the woman, who after recently immigrating to the United States to provide a safer environment for her thirteen-year-old son, suffered a massive brain bleed. Her family sacrificed to bring her home and to provide daily care without the support of services that would have been available to her, had she any insurance and who, despite their efforts, watched her die seven months after coming home. The husband whose wife was given a heart transplant and with that, the promise of a new life, until she contracted COVID and suffered setback after setback. It's impossible to forget the sound of his voice, begging to be let in to visit his wife when visitation restrictions would not allow for it. The fifty-five-year-old man, admitted for treatment of a stroke related to his Parkinson's disease, tearfully recounting a moving bedside visit from his childhood sweetheart, his first love, after years and years of separation. The woman who had hoped to find a cure for her cancer, but was thwarted by housing insecurity, insurance barriers and a hospital bureaucracy that failed her. The young man whose family was told to prepare for his death, only to have him wake up and remove the breathing tube he no longer needed, making a recovery nobody expected. The people who despite strained or fractured connections try their best to meet the moment when their family member is ill; those who mourn the loss of missed opportunities, when someone who never gave of themselves in the ways one might hope while alive, dies without resolution. The countless acts of love and faith, the declarations of hope, wonder and gratitude that our patients and their families can often offer one another and when we are lucky, extend towards those of us who hope to care for them. These moments large and small are now a part of my experience, I carry them with me and am shaped by them in ways I never anticipated.

Hospital work can be grinding and unforgiving. There is little time to stop and reflect; there is always more to do in a day that can realistically be accomplished. It can be hard to tolerate the failings of our health system or bear witness to so many personal tragedies across one professional lifetime. And yet, there is so much to gain when resisting the urge to tamp down our humanity or to callous over, in a failed effort to guard against vulnerability. With each new interaction, I have learned so much, been forever changed for the better, come to understand myself and the world a bit more and expanded my capacity for love; and it is these experiences, that above all else, will be the legacy of this work in my life.

Abigail Latimer

A Palliative Social Worker's Plight

Tears…family discord…imminent decisions…
Team dynamics…personalities…elevated egos…
Fee for service…non-billing…non-essential.

avigating a healthcare system in an under-utilized and understaffed role while providing a misunderstood or outright refused service is a challenge. So naturally, we feel frustrated, but our social work training prepared us for this, right? We were taught to advocate in the face of resistance. We were taught the need to speak out and take our seats at the table as an expert in our field. The thing is nobody said it would be this hard.

The relentless struggle to be heard, respected, and considered an integral team member can be exhausting. We sit at the bedside with patients listening, reflecting, and responding to suffering—only moments later to be ignored and dismissed by administrators, other providers, and sometimes our own team members. We may have confidence in what we are trained to do and what we know we are good at. We *know* that what we provide is essential.

Nevertheless, there is this tremendous amount of dissonance when interacting with the powers that be. The harsh reality is that enterprises dedicated to building healthcare monopolies have little room and patience for services deemed non-reimbursable.

Maybe there is another social worker on the team or in the hospital who *gets it*. Maybe there is a nurse or physician champion who walks with us, defending our position and space. Maybe there is a chaplain who feels equally unheard and does their best to hear us.

But maybe not.

So, we find ourselves in situations not unfamiliar to the social work profession as a whole. Urging those with power to acknowledge our existence, pay us fairly, and give us the ability to care for our patients the way we know how. We decide which battles to take on that day and which ones we will let go of for another day.

For some of us, we leave. We change jobs or organizations. Some of us walk away from the profession altogether—and THAT IS OK. But ultimately, we have to decide what is best for ourselves, and the choices may not be easy or fair.

I will not leave you, reader, with a toxically cheerful ending or call to action. We have heard it all, and quite frankly, I am tired of the empty motivational, albeit placating, messages.

I will leave you acknowledging the hardship and sincerely appreciating everyone who takes it on just for the opportunity to ease another's suffering.

What a social work thing to do.

Vickie Leff

Walled Off

I
t is the job: Listening, watching, absorbing the sorrow, anger and frustration of the patients and families I'd worked with. It feels useful, helpful, even occasionally transformative over these many years.

It wasn't the twenty-two-year-old who died slowly from a gunshot wound that shattered his life and family; the beloved mother of an eleven-year-old girl planning for who would take care of her after her Mom died, or the wry sense of humor from the gentleman who infuriated the staff with his "non-compliance."

It was the loss of my friend of forty-five years who died a slow and deteriorating death from a brain tumor that made me understand how I had conveniently and systematically walled myself off from the death, grief and suffering over the past thirty years of practice in serious illness care. My reactions to illness and death had become wonderfully hidden under a well shellacked sense of humor and sarcasm that could bite (and protect me) through any situation.

I just hadn't noticed how much it shielded me until then, when my friend died. It seemed like I finally felt the callous that had hardened over many cases, helping me to do the work. I didn't (couldn't) really cry when I got the news she had died. It didn't shock me or take me aback. It was another death, like the others—except it wasn't. I wanted desperately to cry.

The moment my hard shell became impenetrable was subtle but weirdly profound. Years ago, working for many weeks with a young woman and her family in the intensive care unit after her heart transplant had gone very and gravely wrong, I thought *this time* I'd be able to impact the horrible, predictable outcome—prolonging her death on machines fueled by a whiff of hope that wouldn't succumb to reality. It was one of those tragic (*you can't make this shit up*) cases that involved ten consult teams and ethics, causing a lot of moral distress, spoken and unspoken. Working with the staff, surgeons, management, and ethics seemed useful and helpful to the patient and family. But, at the end, she died as so many patients I had seen before die…family in shock, nurses furious at providing what they felt was futile care, and others quietly faded into the background of another case.

This case changed my somewhat hopeful, jaded outlook from *I can always do something, be present, etc.*, to *My work probably won't make any difference.* I felt heartbroken and incredibly frustrated.

41

When I learned my friend, whom I had met in college forty-five years ago, had been diagnosed with a Glioblastoma, I wasn't devastated. In fact, I selfishly thought, *oh, I know how this goes, I can help, this is familiar work.* But of course, it wasn't. It was surreal, I felt numb and still do. I regret several conversations with her, and some with her husband, when I adopted a "professional" voice while we talked about "their situation".

My heart just wasn't where it used to be. It was hidden behind a wall that I needed then. Maybe that wall would slowly come down if I contributed to another area of the field. It felt more meaningful to teach, stepping back from the bedside. I wish I could say that everything turned out great and I was able to find the joy in the direct work again. But, I knew it was time to work my way out of clinical care.

Maybe it is in teaching where these experiences will become meaningful and joyful again.

Meagan Lyon Leimena

Being Seen

As we sit across from each other, I listen to their dreams for a family. The excitement of preparing their house and planning to share their lives with children, voices full of retrospective anticipation and joy. Their story evolves into recurrent miscarriages— painful stumbling blocks in their plans. I notice she is looking increasingly tense. Similarly, he keeps inching closer to her until they appear like one figure on the couch, his arm protectively wrapped around her. She explains the last pregnancy was going well, and it seemed like it was going to end in a longed-for baby they would bring home. They smile at each other in their remembrance. Then screening in the second trimester revealed a devastating diagnosis. Shuddering through the details, she recounted that the medical team shared that this baby would live a short, difficult, painful life and surely die quickly. I cringed before I could stop myself, considering the anticipated experience for this baby, and I worried about adding to their pain.

Reminding me how wanted this child was, and with a sharp inhale she said:

"We decided to terminate the pregnancy."

As she weeps, she reminds me she was showing and feeling the baby move by that time. He squeezes her shoulders and looks down. It feels like he is acknowledging the mutuality of their loss, and the singularity of her experience that he cannot truly know. Then, she holds her breath.

I sat in our silence, trying to hold all of the emotions between us. I consider the cruelty of life ending where it is just beginning, and the physical, mystical experience of a parent carrying it all within their body. I am trying to stay with them, in their nearly palpable anguish, fear of judgment, of being unseen in the depths of their pain and the meaning they are seeking out of their losses.

I looked hard at them and their tender rawness. They are parents without a child, deeply wounded and mourning, and I wanted my words to acknowledge this.

When ready, I offer "It sounds to me like you made the best decision for your family. That in your choice, you were parenting your child as best you could. I think you were being the best parents you could be for your child."

"Yes." she sighed and sagged, visibly slumping. The retelling seemed to have deflated her. As if my offering were grace granted, rather than grace shared. They seemed relieved to be addressed as parents, a status denied in their everyday lives.

Before I realized it was happening, two big tears rolled down my face. I smiled sheepishly and wiped them away, trying to acknowledge my feelings without centering them. I felt buried, yet easily activated sadness about my own pregnancy losses, and the babies that were not to be. I felt deep gratitude for the children I have the privilege of parenting. I tried to imagine the incomprehensibility of feeling the kicks of a baby who would never live outside of me. My tears reflected the anguish of their choices, and the wondering about what I would have done in their circumstances. What choice would be more bearable for me, for us? And how would I want to be received as I made my way through life integrating my losses, living without my baby who never grew to be a child or adult? The idea of someone governing these decisions, or condemning them, washed over me with new horror. These thoughts mixed with a primal, guilty relief of having never met these choices personally.

This couple has stayed with me. I think of them as our national discourse rages about pregnancy terminations and the right to make decisions about bodies and families. I remember their deep longing and love for a child they would not have, and the choices they made to be the best parents they could, in the short time they had together. I wish for

45

them the continued grace of being seen for the brave parents they are.

Michael A. Light

Nurturing Intimacy

As an outreach palliative care team dedicated to serving people experiencing homelessness, we work at a unique intersection of suffering. It's a place of daily hardship and loss where towering barriers bring death more often, more swiftly, and sometimes more painfully than for more resourced neighbors. Disproportionately, it impacts people who have faced trauma and oppression for much of their lives, if not generations—a marginalized place where stigma, biases, and fractured health systems are life limiting.

Caring for people affected by great inequity has challenged my capacities and my spirit. I've had to explain that resources for basic survival were not available. I've fought and failed to help patients who use substances receive adequate pain control. I've battled policies which ultimately denied life-saving treatment for a lack of housing and caregivers. I've seen the confluence of patients' limited coping skills and providers' limited de-escalation skills deter the course of critical care. But when the moral distress of these realities compels us to turn away—to detour, depersonalize, discharge, and move on—we risk failing our patients and diminishing our own humanity. When we lean away from rather than into this suffering, we miss opportunities to heal others, ourselves, and the moral shortcomings of society.

Nurturing an intimacy with suffering has helped me befriend the lifelong companions of impermanence and grief. It has also nourished a practice of gratitude that appreciates the joys in this work amidst the moments of deep rage and sorrow. Foremost, it brings me into genuine relationship with people I'm unlikely to meet in other spheres of my life, often at profound periods in their lives. In this shared space, they have become my greatest teachers of survival, resilience, forgiveness, compassion, and love. They have helped me to better understand my role as a clinician and, more importantly, offered perspectives which have altered my view of the world and of myself.

The instances of awe in this work are innumerable. While helping a patient craft a personal statement for what became a posthumous art show, he reflected that "If you give [art] space in your heart, you can't carry animosity or hate." While struggling to keep an apartment or medical appointments, he created art as a divine calling to inspire peace, made in the same public spaces where he was a victim of violence.

I've sung with a patient who wrote music to honor her family, express gratitude to her medical team, and encourage women to seek cancer screening and care despite cultural barriers. "Cancer, you've got nothing on me!" was a battle cry to a disease which claimed generations of women in her family and community. After years of moving to escape violence, she created a home without a house, connections around the world, and an album to promote the power of her message.

I mourned with a man who made a pact to attend substance use treatment if his friend would pursue treatment for lung cancer. Their relationship transitioned from mutual aid while living outside, to mutual support through treatment, to end-of-life caregiving in an apartment we helped them secure. Months after our patient's death, the friend reflected that his own sobriety, housing, and hope for the future were born from the terminal diagnosis of a man he dearly loved and lost.

Recently, a patient emailed me from the van he calls home, en route to see friends before his quickly approaching death. He included a story he wrote about his beloved and departed dog, sharing "life and goodness can be celebrated. That somehow, she can live forever on these pages." I speak and write about my patient with a similar hope—to celebrate the legacies of people which are richer than the resources we have collectively denied them. I share their stories so that others might appreciate their humor, their wisdom, and their values and perhaps lean closer into suffering with compassion. I tell their stories to sustain me in this work and ground my humanity. I tell them to remind myself to see the sacred in every person. I tell them with the hope that they become part of the story that will be told of me.

Sheri Mila Gerson

Connection, Care, and Community

To truly be a healer, one must face the reality that life is impermanent, and that everyone we know will die. I have contemplated death for most of my conscious life, so when I decided to go to social work school in the mid-1980s, I imagined I'd be working with people coping with grief and facing death.

While working as a social worker in a major city in a program that identified people as homeless, I met a man in his thirties who appeared very sick. He agreed to let me take him to a clinic, where after diagnostic tests, he was told by a tearful doctor that he had cancer throughout his body, with no option for treatment that would extend his life. I did what I could to find him housing and care needed for the remainder of his life. In the few months that followed, I visited him frequently, and through a series of auspicious events, was able to locate and help him reunite with family he had been estranged from for several years. During one of my visits, he suddenly looked up, reached up to my face, said thank you, turned over and took his last breath. I went out into the hall to alert staff that he had died. They then

51

proceeded with resuscitation to try to bring him back to life. I knew he was dead, no longer in his body, yet he had no order indicating he did not want resuscitation, and few social workers at the time were educated on what that might mean for someone so young with a serious illness. I left wondering what it means to be alive one moment, dead the next, followed by extraordinary unsuccessful efforts to get a heart beating once again and this wondering has led me to a life of advocacy for and with people facing end of life.

I've learned that we cannot decide what is a comfortable, good, self-determined dying, and wonder if that is the goal. Living and dying are as different as the diversity of the colors and shapes on this planet, but access to care and options for living and dying are limited and for the very few. So many of us are isolated and alone, with few options for care whether it be from family or paid caregivers. There are not enough of us to take care of us. Being with people of all ages, living and dying, makes me reflect on the importance of connection, care, and community.

Arden O'Donnell

Why I Do this Work

My occupation is not conducive to light, surface-level conversations. As a palliative social worker, I spend my days caring for people who are struggling to find meaning in the reality of living with a life-limiting illness, supporting their family members and caring for a medical team who lose the majority of their patients.

When I tell people what I do, the most common question is "How do you do that work?" And some days, I question that myself, but most days I know—I don't focus on the losses, but on the gains. But the real answer of *how*, is found in the *why*. Even on the hardest days, I leave work grateful to have a job that feels like a calling.

I find meaning in the various roles I play:

A temporary guide, offering support and direction on a portion of their illness journey, allowing the space for questions of 'why me' and 'what if?'

A capable translator, asking clarifying questions, decoding the medical terminology, bridging communication across cultural differences and power dynamics.

A patient listener, knowing that acceptance of one's mortality comes slowly, meandering through disbelief, shock, anger, denial, hope, despair, and acceptance.

A silent witness, being present in the meetings when the white coats reluctantly say, "we have done all we can do." I remain behind to console, to restate, to hold space for disbelief.

A supportive colleague, finding the doctor who led an emotional and difficult meeting, knowing they too have a heavy heart and need support.

After over a decade in this work, I feel at home. Words flow freely, my compassion is genuine, and I am comfortable in the care I provide. And yet, there is no way to avoid contemplating my own mortality as I traverse the land of the dying. On these mornings fear overtakes me, and I am convinced that my mild sore throat is a clear sign of an emerging cancer.

The patients who have taught me the most are those who have lived their lives fully until they could not. They embrace the complexity of being human, allowing themselves to be angry, endure treatments that cause pain to get more time, and desperately wish they could stay longer. They mourn lost opportunities, write letters to future grandchildren and are grateful for the life they have had.

They accept their fate in time to reflect on their lives. They have taken inventory, tallied up their accomplishments and failures, told people they love them, asked for forgiveness and most especially forgiven themselves. There is little drama at the end because they have made and shared their conscious choices about how they want to spend their last days.

The team of compassionate clinicians I work with also drive the *why*, underneath the *how* I do this work. These veiled healers' center the humanity of our patients. They listen, advocate and advise, skillfully weaving recommendations that align the patients' values with the medical options available in a failing healthcare system. It is an honor to guide, to translate, to witness, to listen and to support. I feel lucky to have a job that reminds me to live each day fully and provides clarity on how I hope to die.

I Want to Die with Dignity

I want to die with dignity,
under a handmade quilt
sewn by someone who loves me.
I will not shrink into the white hospital sheets
with no trace of the life I lived.
I want to stand on the edge of life and death,
spirit shining through my eyes,

with a knowledge that I gave what I could,
feeling a clear unwavering pride
in the imperfect life I lived.

I want to be the patient who has the power
to wiggle through the boundaries
of medical speak and latex gloves,
to touch the humanity
of those who care for me.
I want to take my last breath,
surrounded by those who love me.
Letting go...
confident that my death
is as important to my life
as my birth.

Chris Onderdonk

Horror, Heartbreak, and the Unshakeable Love

I'm sitting next to Tony in the surgical intensive care unit doing my best to make out what he's writing. He's intubated and I've just asked him, "what's the hardest part of all this?"

He writes out, "I just don't understand why I'm not getting better."

This is my first meeting with Tony. There's a good reason he can't understand why he isn't getting better. He's twenty-four years old. He has terminal cancer. Despite all the best treatment the tumor continues to grow. This is simply not supposed to happen to someone so young. Of course, he doesn't understand.

I pause after reading his words. At this point I've been a palliative care clinical social worker for twenty years. You'd think the most therapeutic words would just roll off my tongue. Instead, I'm struck by sadness. I take a brief moment to gather myself.

"Tony, I don't understand either. I wish we knew why."

Two months after meeting Tony, our team is invited into his room during a dressing change. I'm not prepared for what I see. His tumor has continued to grow leading to a sizable wound. He's being physically disfigured by his cancer. Edges of his skin are eroding.

I feel horrified by what the cancer is doing to him. I'm also feeling overwhelmed and completely heartbroken mustering every ounce of my training and experience to avoid revealing to Tony my reaction to his appearance.

While driving home Tony's wound keeps flashing in my mind. I arrive home, walk through the front door, and am greeted by my family: My wife Tessa and two daughters, Sage and Nico, ages thirteen and ten. Nico, my ten-year-old, immediately starts telling me about the art project she completed. As she's talking, I can tell I'm not present. I've missed half of what she's said. I've had this experience before after certain intense days at the hospital where the transition from horror and heartbreak to kid's art projects is especially jarring. I haven't left the image of Tony behind. He's here. In my living room. I do my best to listen to what Nico's saying but I'm somewhere else.

I've developed a practice for moments like these. I tell my family I need a moment to get out of my work clothes and get dressed. During this time, I practice grounding techniques I've learned in my personal therapy to become present. After getting dressed I practice the techniques and shift my focus to being a dad and husband through the evening.

In our next visit we arrive again during Tony's dressing change. This time it's Tony's mother performing the dressing change. I watch as she patiently and consistently places one piece of white gauze after another into Tony's wound. There's a calm about his mother's demeanor. She's being so gentle and loving in tending to him. It's truly beautiful to witness this act of motherhood. Suddenly I'm feeling awe in the presence of Tony's mother's love and there's a shift in my mood from tension to peace.

I arrive home that evening. I walk through the front door. It's quiet. I stop to notice the stillness in the living room.

I knock on my daughter Sage's door, and she says, "Come in."

I lay down on her bed next to her desk where she's playing Minecraft on her computer. I watch as the flickering light from the computer screen dances across her freckled cheeks. She glances over at me finally noticing that I'm watching her. Our eyes meet.

"Hey daddy, how was your day?"

I notice time standing still. I'm overcome by this sensation of profound love and gratitude for Sage and this moment with her.

I respond, "Actually, today was a really good day."

She replies, "I'm so happy to hear that."

My visit with Tony today has me fiercely present with my daughter, savoring this moment and drinking it all in. It also has me realizing the love in Tony's family being present no matter what the cancer brings. And it's got me feeling the kind of love that will carry my family and I through whatever this life brings through our door.

Shirley Otis-Green

Embracing Ambiguity

My family attended a rural village church that offered the handful of congregants clear guardrails defining acceptable and unacceptable behaviors. And although I could see how these prescriptions provided a degree of comfort to the members, I found them deeply problematic. Somehow, I always found myself focusing on the many shades of gray I saw in the black and white world described by the various preachers who rotated through our tiny community.

As a teen, I was publicly admonished to "Trust in the Lord with all thine heart; and lean not unto thine own understanding" (Proverbs 3:5-6, King James Bible), as the minister could see that I was questioning church authority. Try as I might, I found myself unable to quiet the murmurings of my heart. My parents didn't understand this desire to explore different paths and points of view. Friends worried that I wouldn't be able to navigate life in a city and secretly, I wondered if they might be right. It took all the courage I had to apply to college and later to move out of state for my first job in social work.

That first job was as an Alternate Care social worker for special needs foster children, and I quickly realized that the prescriptions of the bureaucracies that were supposed to be serving these families paralleled the prescriptions of the religious dogma that I had resisted as a child. Clearly (it seemed to me), our systems weren't designed to recognize the many shades of gray represented by those we were to care for, and I couldn't stay long in a system that sought to compartmentalize people into designated boxes for those who would be reunited with their children, and those who wouldn't.

Over the decades, my career has taken a series of unexpected turns, as I've sought to better understand the nuances of life in a multifaceted world. There have been numerous times when I trembled, terrified that the next steps had no signage, and I had no map. But the willingness to explore uncertain paths has opened doors to the most amazing opportunities and led me to places that I would never have imagined. I've richly benefited from colleagues who have emerged as guides and mentors helping me navigate these uncharted spaces. Sitting at the bedside of those facing serious illness is a reminder of the myriad ways people navigate these same uncharted spaces. As a palliative social worker, I've learned the importance of presence when people are struggling with transition and loss, and that we all do better when we are able to increase our tolerance of ambiguity...for indeed, the world is filled with infinite shades of gray.

Arika Moore Patneaude

Surviving Social Work So White*

ocial justice is in my DNA, in the core of my being. It is epigenetic, it is spiritual practice passed down from my Jewish, Native and Black ancestors. It is reparations I pay for their survival of innumerable attempts to eradicate them. Social justice is the homeland that was stolen from us, the center to which I must attend. I had hoped to find this present in the field of social work.

Rather, what I discovered in a field I love, a field that I am *obligated* to critically examine, is that social work often *replicates* the tenets of white supremacy; of control, of hierarchy, of othering, of "-isms" that fuel the churning of its wheels. This realization and the grief associated, infuses the space in which I have felt, at times, smothered by white supremacy, the field of social work.

The field was created by "nice white ladies", not to support those of us whose identities were *intentionally* excluded and marginalized in gaining true self-determination, but rather to position us closer to whiteness as an exchange for access to much needed resources. Basic

64

resources, food, shelter, clothing, healthcare that could only be accessed when we "go along to get along", "yes ma'am", "yes sir", the "man" in order to get access to basic needs. To "gatekeep" access to assistance, to control how we presented ourselves; what we "deserved" to receive was determined by how we looked and acted. To not appear "agitated", or "difficult" or "angry" or "resistant" or "guarded" because we do not want to, or cannot, prostrate who we are at the feet of a gatekeeper, to be tokenized or judged or denied no matter what we do.

Yet, it is understanding that in spite of the unsaid requirements to assimilate, acculturate, position oneself closer to whiteness in order to gain access, built within the foundation of social work is the requirement to question, to counter, to advocate, to engage in social justice and dare I say *decolonize* systems and disciplines such as our own.

To undo the harms of the past, against the Black single mother needing access to resources for her family, for her children, yet a home visit by a person called a social worker meant they were going to look under her bed, or in her closet, in her bathroom for men's shoes, toiletries, or clothing which would negate her access to the much needed resources.

To undo the harm done to our Indigenous relatives that stole generations long traditions essential for living, loving, surviving. Being forced to access resources that would not be needed had the land upon which we lived and thrived not been pillaged and colonized by whiteness.

We must undo harm, UNDO HARM! To counter what I have heard from white social workers, "are you the interpreter?", "YOU have a master's degree?" What was said to me by a seasoned social worker when I applied to graduate school in my early thirties "You'll definitely get accepted, they need to pad their diversity numbers to look good", as if somehow my skin color outweighed my contributions, my intelligence, my well-thought-out admissions essay, and my application.

My undoing of harm is through existing, taking up space, elevating voices that have been marginalized, silenced, discarded, and excluded. Undoing harm is working towards creating a field in which the misconceptions of what a social worker has historically been lessens and hopefully one day no longer exists.

This is my role, my calling, my *future* swan song as one of a small percentage of people of color, of Black people specifically, who are social workers. It is my duty to show future generations of people of color, new social workers or those who might choose our profession, that ours is truly a discipline of social justice, of inclusivity and that my mere existence proves this to be true and is in and of itself an act of resistance, therefore social justice in action.

*Social Work So White was started as a hashtag created and used by SWCARE's to promote a project raising funds for The Loveland Foundation, a fund to support the cost of therapy for Black women and girls.

Dana Ribeiro Miller

In Sunshine and Storm

It's always sunny when the world is falling apart. It's always sunny when the unspeakable is happening. So often, when books or music videos or movies are showing hard moments, the weather in these scenes matches the moment. Dark stormy skies mimic the emotional upheaval faced by the protagonist, the weather lending a cooperative hand to communicating the emotional tenor. But that's not real life. In real life the sun shines— untethered to the circumstances.

It was sunny the May afternoon when my maternal grandfather came over. I was six, my brother was eight days old, and the family was gathering to have dinner with its newest addition. I still remember the bright sunny blue skies as we walked across the lawn. My grandfather having taken advantage of the early spring weather to prop up a new tree that was struggling to grow. An hour later he would be gone—a massive heart attack at the family dinner table.

It was sunny the day in June when my paternal grandfather succumbed to his long battle with cancer. I remember the sharp contrast between the antiseptic hospital smell and cool interior of his intensive care room and the pop of street noise, summer sunshine, and sticky heat when we walked outside of the large urban medical center. It seemed so impossible that the world was carrying on when ours was ending inside.

It was sunny the day in September when my grandmother died. Years of strokes had robbed her of her personhood, her warm spunky wit, and generous nature, her gentle soul with always a kind word. She spent the last years of her life entrapped by her mind with moments where she shined through enough to be heard. She died on hospice with her family by her side, and her beloved Aretha Franklin singing in her ear. The early fall sunshine there to carry her through. A poignant sunshine, no less painful, no less bright.

I have sat with people in sunshine, and in storms, their pain no less palpable, and their reality no less stark. When I started this work, I hoped to help make this transition somewhat easier for them. I recognize the hubris in that now.

There is no rule book that says death has to be hard or sad. For some death is gentle peace after a long road. For some, there is no path out of the pain of losing a beloved— only through it. For some death is complicated, grief even more so. There is no one experience of death, no one way of coping, no one way of grieving, or not. No one person or intervention can take away the pain or stop the flow of tears.

But one person can be a gentle presence. One person can reframe complex topics in a way a stress frazzled brain can understand. One person can be an advocate, a light post on a journey. One person can highlight systemic injustices still causing harm in the last moment of a life. One person can ask the hard questions or intervene when the questions being asked are too hard. One person can be.

It's always sunny when someone's world is falling apart. Illness waits for no one. Death comes, in the words of my mentor, when the heart stops, no sooner no later. There is no holding on for a beloved, waking up out of sheer will. Death is the one guarantee to arrive on time, on its own schedule, at its own pace. It doesn't wait for a stormy day, it doesn't wait for the blizzard to clear.

Allie Shukraft

How 'The Police' Influenced my Career

Like many in the field of hospice and palliative care, music plays an important role in my work. As an inpatient pediatric palliative care social worker, it can help determine my outlook on the drive in or help me find release after a particularly difficult shift. I can often find lyrics to quote or a well-known tune to reference that pertains to a conversation with a family or teammate. And like many of the Gen-X persuasion, I LOVE to make playlists . . . I make them for teammates when they need a pick-me-up, for patients as a way to stay connected when they are going home after a long hospital stay, or for myself to memorialize a specific experience. But sometimes there is a song that just perfectly sums up an idea and when it comes to my career, even to the field of palliative care, that song is *Synchronicity I* by The Police.

The song is about this intangible, indefinable force in the world, and this is something that we see many days in our work. We see the mysteries of life and death, love and hate, joy and anguish all play out in front of us. In pediatrics, we

71

often see what parents and families attribute as miracles; children living years beyond their prognoses, bodies which science says have so many limitations but which live, (perhaps hope?), shows us otherwise. There are moments in my career when I have arrived in a room just as a parent has asked for me to be called, just as a patient has died, just as a parent has received bad news. I was there when a mother, holding her newly deceased infant, wanted to chase after her upset husband and no one else in the family could hold the baby. I could and had the time to stay. I was also there when a family needed someone to come with them to the operating room for organ procurement for their child, which allowed an extra staff member to be there when Mom needed to step out. Were these, and countless other moments coincidences, or *synchronicity*? I choose the latter.

My second year MSW placement was supposed to be with an adult hospice social worker. She left that role several weeks before the semester started and after some negotiation and shuffling, I ended up with a pediatric hospice social worker, a placement I had never even considered. *Synchronicity*. The social worker at the local hospital's pediatric palliative care team was planning to leave to become a nurse right around the time of my graduation, leaving a vacancy in a position that, at the time, no one wanted. *Synchronicity*. I have been in that job for fourteen years now. There have been moments with patients and families that would fit what The Police sang about—connective tissue bringing us all together, moments where their children speak to ancestors who have already left this plane of existence, often just shortly before their own deaths. These moments are so helpful to parents when they allow themselves to be open to them, when they don't try to force meaning on the experience but rather let the meaning reveal itself.

The same can be said for palliative care as a field and palliative care social work as a career—let the meaning reveal itself to you. If you open yourself to the mystery, the *synchronicity* of this world, you just may find "something inexpressible" that brings you closer to your patients and families, as well as to yourself. Remain curious. Continue to ask people questions, to be curious about them and their families, as well as their hopes and dreams. They will continue to teach you more about themselves as well as revealing real truths about the world to you. If you look for *synchronicity*.

Bridget Sumser

What I Would Tell Her Now

I had just had a baby. Motherhood was new and encompassing and colored everything. I was porous. The hallways of the hospital, so familiar, felt foreign, loud. No longer sterile but alive, the stories which before hid behind doors and curtains overflowed out, making it harder for me to move at the quickened pace that had become second nature. I heard the hushed tones and laughter, the drones of televisions, the beeping of monitors in a way I couldn't feel before.

In becoming a mom, I too had been born into a new life. Emotion was at the surface. I was both softer and less flexible, unsure how to hold all that had moved through me before. I knew how to be affected in brief bursts, but now, my senses were flooded. My body had felt defined, contained amidst loss. Now, I felt like water.

Sheefa had lived with cancer since she was a teenager. She came into the hospital almost weekly for unmanageable pain and everyone thought she needed to talk to me because by not making eye contact she was read as "angry." Sheefa didn't want to talk to me. And honestly, I don't know how much I wanted to talk to her. I felt scared, affected, unsure.

I stopped by many times before Sheefa was ready to be with me in any way. I'd knock, announce myself, and she'd reply "not now" letting us both off the hook. But one day, it changed. "Wanna sit down, Ms. Bridget?" I did and felt a relief that was unexpected. There we were, on her time, which really was our time, because I was more available, too. I don't know what we talked about that day. I remember the sun coming through the window and landing on my back, her face. It was warm in the room. It was fall and the leaves were changing, and the clouds moved quickly across the sky.

It was the beginning of something.

"Will you talk to me about being a mom?" she asked me a year later. She stared into my eyes, almost asking "is this ok?" I stared back, blinked tears to the sides of my eyes, feeling the warmth of the sun on my legs in order to catch my breath. I didn't know what to say.

I had talked to Sheefa weekly. We had become—not friends—but we loved each other. I no longer lingered at her door. I walked straight to her bed, sat down into our time. She told me of her boyfriend, her struggles with her mom, her longing for normalcy, her hopes for a future that wouldn't be. I told her about my son Noah and eventually the pregnancy I could no longer hide under my oversized dress.

Sheefa tracked Noah, "our baby" as she called him, better than some of my friends. One afternoon as we sat together reviewing plans to get her out of the hospital, she stopped. "I need to know what it feels like to care for a baby. My arms feel—empty." With her words, the light stood still, the air didn't dare move. There we were in the kind of deep truth that leaves you breathless. My body effervescent, adrenaline coursing down my heavy, pregnant limbs.

What would I tell her about being a mom? A year after her death—ten months after my daughter's birth—I would tell her my heart is bigger, squishier, more vulnerable. Being a mom means being open to occasional moments of truth that stop everything. For me, it means learning to hold expanding life as fluently as I have held lives in review, lives contracting to a close. I would tell her she helped me come to understand the space I need to be the mother I want to be for my children. I would tell her that while my daughter's name is Uma, somehow, unconsciously, in the winding poetic flow of nicknaming in my family, I started calling her Shaba which morphed to Sheesh which transformed to Eefa. I would tell her, I didn't know how to answer you then, but I can now.

Laurel Tropeano

The Risks in Being *Real*

In the beginning, I was terrified to be uncovered as a fraud. I was someone who didn't understand the systems, the dilemmas, and the lived experience of suffering. I was sure that the words coming out of my mouth would give me away. Slowly, miraculously, one story at a time, one follow-through at a time, one clinical choice at a time, I became *Real*.

But—also like Pinocchio—every time I have let a patient or family down, I have felt these mistakes to be written all over my face. My joy and relief in being *Real* is tempered by my realization that, as it turns out, it's hard to be human. Some days I don't have *It*. Some days I am tired, sad, distracted, hungry, and cowardly.

On those days, I rely on both my faith and the knowledge that the pendulum will swing back. I will again experience that song in my soul when I have relaxed into the zone, into learning about the person I am serving, the system we are navigating together, or the disease barreling down. I will again feel the magic of connecting on the deepest level with someone. I will again dance easily on the knife's edge between knowing and not-knowing. What makes these days possible, paradoxically, is that I will bring what I have learned from the less-than days. Instead of pretending they don't exist, I will call on them because they keep me human, (and actually make me better at seeing the humanity it all). Being *Real* means bringing every one of our Selves to the party.

I feel such deep respect for the consistent bravery of the patients and families we all serve—even, or especially, at times when they feel the least brave. If they can show up, I can show up.

This is scary, the work we are doing, because we have to be willing to use our *Real Selves* in a world we can't control. We know we will experience pain, and with that the greatest joys of our lives.

Clara Van Gerven

Why Is There a Social Worker Here?

When I introduce myself to the couple—a clinic patient and his wife—she asks, "why is there a social worker here?" It's a good question. Why *am* I here? It's a question I revisit constantly. It followed me on those first forays into palliative care in my advanced field placement, those first times I ventured into rooms by myself; and now – it follows me from room to room.

Before I got tossed into the deep end of the interprofessional pool, I remember reading the research on interprofessional teams suggesting that medical social work suffers from a lack of role definition. It checks out. Working in a hospital teaches you no one has time for fluff, which makes it the best and also worst place to learn where you fit in. During my social work fellowship, I worked with a woman dying of poorly controlled HIV. Confused at times, angry a fair bit. Her adult daughter asked me, essentially, what was going on, and whether there was going to be more treatment. I don't even remember what I told her, but here's what I didn't do: I didn't set up a family meeting; I didn't ask the medical team to help her (or me!) to understand. Instead, I spent time with the daughter, trying to help her understand the situation, trying to work on the incomplete support system that was part of why her mother was in the hospital. I tried really hard not to make a nuisance of myself to the overworked palliative team and flapped like an anxious puffin around the increasingly aggravated family.

When I finally asked for help, my infinitely kind rotation social work mentor immediately involved one of the palliative physicians, and the primary team, and set up a family meeting; all on a Friday afternoon as I was about to go off rotation, meaning I was leaving my team with all this mess. I wasted days and days when I could have been getting the concrete answers this family was looking for.

It's just one example of a very long list of times when I stood in the hallway wondering what the hell I was doing and how I was ever going to figure that out. It's hard being a learner when so much is at stake.

And they ask *why palliative care*? With faces full of baffled aversion. What I want to say is: *what better place for terrifying vulnerability? When everyone is raw and tender like a new bruise, can I bring bare humanity, bare listening?* That, and maybe a cup of ice chips, a warm blanket, and ice cream. People love ice cream. This much I've learned: bring trustworthiness, kindness, and ice cream.

In among a tidy set of well-defined professions, palliative social workers bring the messy tool of *me*, our whole selves. It's complicated, bringing the whole catastrophe of oneself to work. The constant self-reflection this entails is something that social workers are well trained for, and which is also unbearably slow and cumbersome. That moment when you are driving home from work and think— how did I not see that before? And the sigh when you realize you're going to have to fix it.

Over time, with the good fortune of great social work mentors and great colleagues of different disciplines, the response to the question *what am I doing here* becomes both clearer and more nuanced. It also becomes more seamless as those squeaky new clinical skills become more silently automatic, like that first time you merge onto a highway without noticing. One day a patient's brother looks me in the eye and says, "I didn't even notice you doing that, that's good." The truth is that I didn't notice either, and that whatever skills I bring are only effective to the extent that I am authentic.

The paradox is this: Quiet discernment is loud and clunky to develop. Sometimes my learning will leave marks on others. If there's a way around that I clearly haven't found it.

Cara L. Wallace

When We See Ourselves: Reflecting on Personal and Professional Connections

It was a normal Tuesday morning in November, a crisp breeze causing me to pull my jacket closer to me as I walked to the front door of my newest hospice patient, a thirty-seven-year-old woman with stage four metastatic breast cancer. Her mother answered the door. As I stepped into the warm foyer of the home, I was greeted by a large wedding portrait of a young bride. Her mother looked up at it as I did, remarking in a hushed tone,

"She was so vibrant then. She looks nothing like that now."

She led me back to a quiet bedroom, where Laura laid in bed with a winter hat covering her head, warm blankets pulled up to keep her warm. She greeted me with a smile and after introducing myself we talked about her life, her fears, and her family.

She worried most about her young children—would they remember her? Would they be okay when she was gone? I shared some resources with her, for her logistical care and current needs, and to provide support for her family—her husband, kids, and parents who were staying with them. We also talked about resources that would be available for them following her death. I spoke once more with her mother before I left and made plans to visit again later at a time when others would also be present.

When I arrived home for the day, my visit from that morning with Laura stayed with me. I had only recently discovered that I was pregnant with my first child, not yet detectable to others but persistently obvious to me by changes within my body and my emotions. I wondered what it must be like to be Laura, to face death knowing she would not have the opportunity to see her young children grow up. Her wedding portrait reminded me so much of my own— one gifted to me by my parents, stored away since my modest home did not have a space befitting of its grandeur. There was something about our two portraits that connected us—both vibrant young brides imagining our futures as a wife and mother. She, too, had worked in healthcare.

After years of clinical practice, it's strange the way certain moments affix themselves independently in our memories, while others flitter away only to be remembered in congregate with similar patients and stories. I think often about the power of our own stories and experiences.

Though historically, clinicians have been taught to separate themselves from their professional experiences, they are in fact intimately intertwined with our personal ones. We must provide space for ourselves to reflect on these connections, to support ourselves through our own emotional responses, and to consider how they impact our clinical work with patients and families. Finding this space is a matter of ethical imperative. Failure to do so, denies opportunity for supporting our own well-being and self-care, and creates potential for unintentional outcomes in our provision of care.

WINDOWS

Andrew Wyeth: Looking Out, Looking In. National Gallery of Art 2014.
Wind From the Sea, 1947 (public domain)

Esther Ammon

Entering the Unknown

As I meet my first COVID patient, I enter the unknown. There is a surge of energy as the medical team pushes the hospital bed of Ms. Guzman onto the unit. This feels different. This is unmistakably distinct. I can feel the unease as everyone works to get her stabilized. Ms. Guzman's husband is in a similar state at another hospital: critical condition, intubated and sedated with an uncertain prognosis. We learn that her adult son, Alejandro, is in quarantine at home. Thankfully he is recovering and with this we breathe a collective sigh of relief. Ms. Guzman is getting worse. Visitation policies seem to change by the minute. For each new update there are multiple new questions: Will the family be able to visit? Does her son need to be cleared by the health department? Are there exceptions for patients who are at the end of life? Is she really at the end of life?

As a social worker I am made for this. It is my call to arms! Precipitating event, intervention, stabilization and so forth... but I ask myself, how can I help when I am also having difficulty coping? I try to avoid it, but patients, families and staff all seem glued to an endless stream of fear-inducing news on the TVs in the intensive care unit. The tension is palpable. There is no time to pause and reflect. Finally, Alejandro is cleared to come to say good-bye. Doubt re-surfaces, *will he make it in time? Are we sure he isn't still contagious?* As he stands, glued against the glass of the negative pressure room, staring at his beloved mother, he weeps. In full personal protective equipment, the chaplain and I are frozen, six feet apart, glancing back and forth at him and then each other. We can't even touch him. How are we supposed to support him? This is our job, after all. They are Catholic. He asks for Holy Water. I watch the nurse and priest in awe as they coordinate over the phone, through the glass. The priest coaches her through the ritual, speaking back and forth to her and then to Alejandro. I feel so helpless, maintaining my distance as the son sobs. He is all alone. It feels so cruel.

As social workers we are taught that we cannot fix things; that bearing witness *is* an intervention. Yet, I find myself unable to stand still. I need to do *something*. I constantly ask myself *will any of this help?* In consultation with Infectious Disease I receive permission to have clay fingerprints of Ms. Guzman made and then meticulously sanitized. At least it is something. A tangible reminder of their shared stories.

For months following Ms. Guzman's death I thought about her and her family. Things continued to change so quickly. Visitation and physical distancing became less strict. Every time the chaplain and I saw each other we would give one another a knowing look: almost as though we were checking in on one another, but rarely were words exchanged as we hustled through the halls. And then I came across an interview online: Ms. Guzman's family describing their experience in the hospital, the trauma they had endured, the powerlessness they felt. Again, I asked myself, *could I have advocated more?* The next time I saw the chaplain I almost told her about the interview. But then I thought, *to what end? We can't change anything now.*

This work has humbled me. There are always new experiences and new challenges ahead. How do we sit with the knowledge that we, too, are only human? There are limits to what we can do. So, while we do our best to hold this truth in our work, we also lean in by asking how else can we learn and grow?

Tracy Borgmeyer

Reflection on Community and Sacrifice

During a COVID surge, with hospital beds at capacity, my coworkers and I were feeling the strain of well over a year of the pandemic. We had a vaccine, widely available by then, that people were still rejecting. At the same time, families whose unvaccinated loved ones were critically ill on ventilators were requesting ineffective treatments, based on social media posts. Symptomatic people still ignored precautions, avoided COVID testing, refused vaccinations, and delayed seeking treatment until it was too late. Many deaths in our area were preventable.

At various times we felt sorrow, disbelief, anger, pity, and even indifference. The patients were adults; they had to make their own decisions and live with the consequences, right? But some were more vulnerable to the misinformation, and even pressure, by others. The spouse of a patient who died, along with thousands of others, had been persuaded by a doctor on social media that high doses of a corticosteroid would cure COVID. The patient whose spouse considered legal action to force administration of

Ivermectin to their critically ill spouse later posted false information on social media increasing requests for Ivermectin based on a deception. There are many more stories I will never forget.

I remembered feeling that frustration and anger during my years in oncology. It was not uncommon for people with cancer to use products they found in natural foods stores or online—vitamin supplements, colon cleanses, colloidal silver, inhaling crystals—and had purchased at significant expense, with credit cards or money they did not really have. The purveyors of these products also used government conspiracies about the Food and Drug Administration, National Institutes of Health, or National Cancer Institute to undermine trust in the healthcare system. Patients would say they heard oncologists don't really want to find cures for cancer, and pharmaceutical companies just want to enrich their shareholders by selling treatments that don't work. Clinical trials were avoided with the comment "I'm not going to be their guinea pig"—the same comments as those who feared the safety of COVID vaccines.

We do have to remember that in the history of medicine, the public trust has been violated, time and again. Today's common practices around informed consent and research participation, for example, were developed in response to gravely unjust and unethical conduct. When the direct harm is over, the mistrust lives on.

But we have a great deal of freedom in our society, and sometimes that means there is very little accountability for the accuracy of information which can be disseminated. Consumers of health-related information must usually scrutinize for themselves. Parallel to one of the most highly regulated healthcare systems in the world, there exists an unregulated media-based ecosystem which operates freely, where culpability for harm is impossible to ensure.

What is our protection against this?

In some cases, it may be possible to hold licensed healthcare professionals responsible. It also helps to have a high level of health literacy in a community, if and when we can. Yet another safeguard may be *community*. Human beings need community, not isolation. Relationships, not screens. Trusted friends and family who tell the truth and who can confront without alienating. Caregivers who feel accountable for those in their care and who are willing to make small personal sacrifices—or even great ones—to protect them. I remember one woman, a caregiver for her parents, who had frightened them about vaccination. Multiple family members and a trusted doctor persuaded the daughter that her parents were better protected by being vaccinated. Despite advanced age and fragile health, they survived severe COVID illness months after being vaccinated. We protect each other when we understand the *common good* and hold it as a higher value than individual freedom—not in every moment of life, but certainly in pandemic, war, and disaster.

This haiku, author unknown, appeared in my inbox around Thanksgiving 2020. Seventeen syllables about sacrifice, the common good, and community.

We isolate now
So when we gather again
No one is missing.

Stephanie Broadnax Broussard

She Looks Like Me

"Brace yourself. She is a tough one, and the daughter can sometimes be difficult. They are a nice family. They just do not get it."

As my colleague prepared to introduce me to the patient in the exam room, she explained that the patient and family have unrealistic expectations and refuse to discuss goals of care or hospice. As I stood in the hallway, I could hear laughter, a deep but familiar tone, and the rhythmic cadence as the patient spoke. Her voice reminded me of the women in my family and community. It felt like a warm embrace as I prepared to enter the room.

The patient was an older Black woman with stage four pancreatic cancer with bone metastasis. She has had multiple lines of chemotherapy. The physician's various attempts to engage in advance care planning and discuss prognosis had been met with resistance and often ended with both parties feeling unheard and frustrated.

It was common for the physician and team to call me in to talk with patients resistant to exploring end-of-life care. I noticed an increased comfort in my team to verbalize their difficulties in communicating with Black patients about the end of life. I wasn't sure if my referrals for these patients and families had increased or if I had become more aware.

She had a beautiful smile. There was an incongruence in her body's frailty and apparent weakness and the sound of vitality in her voice. Accompanying the patient was her daughter, who conveyed a level of distrust in the care team and their intentions. I didn't shy away from discussing her concerns. I validated them. They were layered with her own experiences, historical factors, and familial racial traumas. Many I have personally had to reconcile. We explored what they understood about her condition and clarified where I could.

As I began to go deeper and explore goals and values, she glared at me in a familiar gaze that I had been the recipient of as a child.

"I do not say I have cancer because I am not claiming that, but they are treating me for cancer." Her daughter loudly interjected, "she is not dying, and we do not want to talk about hospice. I am not going to let them give up on her. She is just taking a break from chemo to get stronger."

The daughter's voice shook, the fear and concern were visible in her eyes.

I softly responded, "I can see how much you love her. You are doing a great job advocating. I can only imagine

95

how taxing it has been to feel like the team's goals aren't in line with yours. It is not my job to point you in one direction or another. I want to ensure you know your options and that we clearly understand your direction and goals, so we know how best to care for you."

We discussed the patient's condition, beliefs, values, and goals. We centered the patient's voice but also gave space to her daughter to ensure that we did not negate her role. As time progressed, a sense of familiarity overtook us all. I helped to foster an understanding that there was space for them to exercise and honor their faith while participating in planning and the need for care to coexist. Not only did I gather a better understanding of their perspective, but I also bore witness as they had a beautiful exchange as they both leaned into the vulnerability of the moment and the idea that time was fleeting.

We met once after this initial conversation—the second conversation, I was greeted with warmth and gratitude. The discussion was filled with emotional support, providing clarification, education on hospice services, and dispelling myths. Within one week of our initial meeting, she decided that hospice was best for her and her family. She passed away one month later, in her home, surrounded by family as requested. This experience and so many like it validates and affirms my commitment to improving the experiences of all those living with serious illnesses, but especially those that look like me.

Chelsea K. Brown

Pen to Paper: Honoring Anger & Sadness

A Journal Entry
Jae-
This one's for you.

*I*saw Theo downtown. I walked out of a shop and there he was. Same jacket as always. He saw me, we locked eyes, and then we hugged. He immediately started crying. He told me again about how he didn't get to say goodbye to you. How he didn't even get to see your body after you died. How he just wants to take care of you—even now. He is still trying to raise money for cremation. He is still so kind, even through grief and anger, even after how he was treated.

I wish I knew what was in your heart that Friday afternoon when I left the hospital. But you were in so much pain. Sleepy from needing so much medication. Nothing seemed to help. More than anything, I hoped that Theo would make it to your bedside that weekend. That if he did, they would call off Security and let him stay overnight. I worried you would die that weekend. I knew what mattered to you most was that he would be okay.

I don't think he will ever be "okay" after losing someone as special as you. But he is surviving. And I remember a day when you were worried he wouldn't survive.

So, I had to write and tell you the good news. What a gift to see him after all this time. He is still with us, surviving. And feeling your presence along the way. You are missed.

-C

On this day, I journaled for the first time in ages. I wrote this passage after seeing Jae's partner downtown. I walked back to my apartment filled with restlessness and grief. My skin prickly and my ears buzzing. Flooded with the emotion I felt when Jae eventually died, separated from her partner and utterly alone in the hospital. One year into palliative care and I was feeling a pressure build inside without any space to just…release. Back to writing, I decided.

As I journaled, the memories of Jae and Theo flowed to the surface…

Those weeks caring for Jae were simultaneously devastating and mobilizing. Jae and Theo had been living without housing for years. Jae was white and her partner Theo was Black. As she neared her final days, Theo's grief grew and erupted. Although folks on our palliative team perceived Theo to be grieving, others in the hospital did not interpret Theo's emotion in the same way. Security was called to escort him out of the hospital more than once, claiming that he was a "threat to staff." He was eventually banned from returning—infuriatingly, on the same Friday evening Jae was imminently dying. No amount of advocacy on our team's part was successful at reversing this decision. And yet, how many times had we seen white caregivers yell and curse in despair without Security being called? The answer was sickeningly obvious. I remember leaving the hospital that night with hot tears, unwilling to view this event for anything other than what it was: a racist and violent response to grief and suffering. When would things change?

Now, weeks after Jae's death, I had stumbled across Theo on their same street, trying to raise money for her cremation. He told me the hospital called letting him know that Jae's body would be sent to the county's "group cremation," but he was determined to raise enough money for a spot for her ashes, close to their favorite street.

In our last moment together, we said "goodbye." After the word left my mouth, I felt my body tense. "Goodbye" felt like such a tiny, constricted word. It couldn't possibly hold all my sadness and gratitude for Theo. So, I added "thank you for being Jae's person" and "I'll be thinking of you." Later that evening, as I journaled for the first time in ages, I remembered when Jae used to show me poems she had written—sometimes shedding her anger or sadness. I hoped she would be proud that I was putting pen to paper. I think she would tell me to *make it worth something*. So, I ask myself… what now?

Jennifer Hill Buehrer

Code Blue in a White Boa

I'd been working inpatient palliative care only about a year. There were a couple of people who helped me find my place in the field, and she was one of them. Erica had been a social worker many years longer than I and worked for a local hospice agency. She was tall, beautiful, and radiant, and I looked up to her in just about every way. She made herself available to me anytime, to talk about my role as a social worker in the medical field—something that can be confusing and frustrating.

One day she was admitted to my hospital with symptoms related to a new finding of cancer in her brain. She had been on the rehab unit and came back to the medical floor when her condition deteriorated. I remember meeting with her and her husband, and several specialists whom I rarely saw participate in family meetings to discuss goals of care. This was a patient who brought people together. We made a plan for radiation, leading to more chemo, and talked about code status as a matter of routine. She was young, and vital, and *of course* we would do what we had to do to keep her going, including CPR. Erica couldn't really participate; I can't help wondering if the outcome would've been different if she had.

Having Erica as a patient gave me a chance not only to offer the kind of support and encouragement she'd always given me, but it gave me a glimpse into her personal life. Her husband Robert was a teacher, and as beloved by his community as Erica was by hers. I still carry a photo of her, in her hospital bed, wearing pink pajamas, a white feather boa, and a tiara–with a magic wand in her hand. Friends had brought her these things, because they thought that her medical team needed to see her the way they saw her: Magic. The truth was, we didn't need any of that for us to see her that way.

The day is a bit of a blur for me but at some point that morning I heard overhead, "CODE BLUE on 1 East"—my floor. The oncology unit. I think I knew right away that it was Erica. She'd been having more trouble walking, talking, organizing her thoughts, and there was concern about blood clots. I heard the unit doors burst open and chaos in the hallway. I ran toward it and there they were, in Erica's room, and Robert in the hall. I will never forget the sight of one after another code team member taking turns putting all their weight on Erica's body, over and over again. Her poor, lifeless body bouncing on the bed with every blow. There was blood *everywhere*. I didn't know that happened during a code. Her clothes were off, and everyone in the room... everyone in the hall... saw her naked body as it was being beaten in an attempt to shock it back to life. For what? For more radiation, some chemo, and then... more of this?

All I could do was stand in the hall with Robert, offering comfort. Listening. Now, years later, in this same situation I'm much more apt to speak and ask loved ones if they want us to continue. What do I have to lose, when I know there is no good end to a code like this one? At least we can offer a peaceful death and a chance to say goodbye.

Erica taught me that; I owed that to her. I don't know how long the code went on or even who called it, but I think it was Robert. And I think I encouraged him. That's how I remember it anyway. It was futile from the start. But Erica understood that I needed this learning experience. And gave it to me, as she gave her life. Fifteen years later I am still making it up to her.

Sharon K. Chung

Find Your Song and Sing It

Mas

Mas came onto our service in late January presenting as a forty-year-old, Black male, HIV+, and suffering from uncontrollable pain.

Since late fall, Mas was dealing with pain and despite going through numerous medical workups, a clear diagnosis remained elusive. After another readmission for increased pain and lethargy, a few more tests were ordered, and it became evident that Mas was suffering from AIDS related cancer and symptoms. Mas then disclosed he had been diagnosed with HIV over ten years ago and stopped taking antiretroviral therapy after several years. As medical treatments were then adjusted and Mas' HIV viral load was controlled, it soon became a matter of time to see if Mas' body would respond to on-going treatment as symptoms continued to worsen.

Mas was then referred to palliative care for pain control and goals of care discussions.

Joe

Every time I entered Mas' room, Joe was there. Sometimes reading a book, sometimes on the phone with a friend, often Joe was gently caring for Mas at bedside. Upon entering, Joe's expression would warm, he would often smile, and in an upbeat tone always said, "Hey Mas, look who's here".

Joe was generous in sharing openly about his relationship with Mas. They met and started dating when Joe was working and living in the south. When Joe decided to move back north, Mas wanted to follow Joe, maybe with some hope that he would be more comfortable being out as gay. Joe shared how Mas said he was surprised that after leaving the South, he found that it was easier to be gay but harder to be Black.

Joe shared about himself. Mas never said anything to Joe about his status during their relationship and Mas' health history had never been an issue up until last fall. They were in a committed relationship and had always practiced safe sex. Joe shared that after learning about Mas being HIV+, Joe addressed his own health care concerns and assured me he was okay.

Transition

Mas died the day after Valentine's Day.

A few days earlier, Joe shared that he knew time was

running out for Mas and wanted to support Mas in whatever he wanted. Mas was on the acute rehab floor, awaiting a transfer back to the oncology floor as Mas had life-prolonging goals.

It was late in the day as I walked onto the unit to check on Mas and Joe. The way Mas' nurse greeted me told me Mas' medical status had changed.

Joe was at bedside with Mas, a couple of close friends were also in the room. The doctor came in and explained that Mas' body was giving up and time was now shorter than wanted. Joe made decisions with Mas and Joe graciously invited me to join them as the doctor left the room. We called Mas' mom. We were present as life transitioned to death. The time felt unwanted, felt loving, felt sacred, like time was moving too fast, like time wasn't moving, like time wasn't enough, like time became meaningless.

Life Legacy

Joe, with the heart of love and unconditional acceptance that is him, held a legacy fundraiser honoring Mas. Funds raised benefitted The Aliveness Project, a local non-profit that connects people living with HIV to resources and connections for leading healthy and self-directed lives. During the event, I couldn't help but wonder what life Mas would have lived had he always felt free to be both Black and gay and anything else he wanted to be. How had the ill forces of homophobia and racism shaped a fated path for Mas as he lived his life?

Every week, as it is on his grocery store route, Joe drives by The Aliveness Project. Joe looks through the office window facing the street where a stained-glass art piece titled, "Find Your Song and Sing It" hangs. The stained-glass was created to honor Mas' legacy and a plaque hanging next to the art piece tributes Mas's life. The image is a bird of imagined species, soaring upwards, a red ribbon in its beak, the wings meeting at a V on the bird's lower back. V is for Visibility. V is for Victory over AIDS.

Nancy Cincotta

Remembering Karen

What do we learn about what we may disclose about our personal life to those we work with, and what we do not? When working with people nearing death, I wonder if some of those answers change. I often think about situations in which my responses came from my gut, and not really anything that I would call "learned wisdom."

I had been working with Karen from the time she was diagnosed with rhabdomyosarcoma until she died at age seventeen. She clearly saw me as someone she could talk to about anything and ask any question. As she approached the end of her life, she made a point of telling me that she felt like I was "in this" with her. Her parents had divorced before she was diagnosed, and she had struggled in relationships with them, each in their own way. She wanted to make peace with her parents, but her life was ending, and it was unclear that she would achieve that goal. I encouraged them to talk, to be with each other. I facilitated communication and worked with her to try to achieve her goals.

At one point, Karen was going on in great detail about an altercation with her father. In the midst of her depiction, she sat up and said, "Am I boring you?"

Then she wanted to know, "How can I work this out?"

Time was not on her side. We talked about the fact that there was often a time, in which in the natural order of things, teens and young adults sometimes move away from their parents emotionally and then at later stages, families coalesced and often things worked out.

She wondered if that was the case for me—and it had been. So, I decided it could be helpful to share some of the story of my life. She was near death at this point, but she sat up throughout our conversation (and was not bored!!). In some ways I used my life as a template for what could have happened in her life. The end of that evening's discussions did not resolve the issues Karen was facing, but the conversation actually seemed to help her be more at peace with her reality, her age, and the knowledge that if she were to live longer, things in her life might have followed a more developmentally appropriate course, and if making peace with her parents was the goal, she would likely have achieved that goal.

As death approached, this peace of mind seemed to free her up to think about some of the things she was currently worried about and yielded questions such as, "Could I be buried in the fetal position?" Karen and our conversations have stayed with me. I have written about her and thought about her because in my forty years of practice with children at the end of life, no one else had/or has asked me if they could be buried in a different position. It is also true that very rarely have I used my own personal history as a tool to help someone who will not live to grow up.

Susan Conceicao

Remembering

When asked to contribute a reflection based on my almost thirty years working as a social worker in hospice and palliative care, what first came to mind were "snapshots" (a rather archaic term). I remember walking into my first hospice patient's home on the lower East Side in New York City and falling in love. The patient was a ninety-six-year-old Hispanic woman who lived with her daughter. I don't exactly recall what I did but do remember walking around for weeks afterward telling anyone who would listen how much I loved my hospice patients. What was it? As I reflect backwards, I remember thinking—*Is this God?*—A unique thought from the non-religious me. In more current terms is it an energy, a sacred space, a place of grace, or simply the time in people's lives in which only authenticity, and love remain.

I remember a Jewish hospice residence I was privileged to manage for about three years. I remember how people would get off of the elevator and ask "What is this place?"—a response similar to my first experiences, as it was truly a place of love and compassion. I remember the miracle of getting to love the patients with dementia who could hardly put a sentence together and feeling truly heartbroken when they died. It was a place where the self-pay, well-to-do, the unhoused and persons who society might describe as having checkered pasts received the same beautiful, loving, high quality care.

I started a group which we called a "meeting" which met once a week. The group members included a professor from India, two African American men with histories of substance use, an older Russian speaking man, and several others. The men called the professor "Doc" and treated her with such respect and care.

I remember the Orthodox Rabbi who defied convention and made sure that there was a Christmas tree in the residence so that everyone could celebrate the holiday according to their beliefs and traditions. I remember thinking to myself that we had truly created a microcosm of what the world should be.

As I write this, I realize that what has kept me going all of these years in a field that is at times frustrating, at others heartbreaking, is love. These memories live in me and are there to call on at moments of doubt, tiredness, or questioning.

Jill P. Farabelli

With a Fierce and Kind Heart

People often ask me how I started working in palliative care. My responses typically range from something like "good question" to "the field found me". As I reflect on this question for myself after a year of many difficult patient losses, I no longer think it matters how I got here—it's more about the reasons I stay.

Jack was a young man diagnosed with metastatic cancer. He had it all—loving, dedicated wife, two beautiful children and an impressive career. Two years after diagnosis, he took his last breath.

The last few months of his life the disease continued to spread, despite aggressive cancer treatment. Jack became physically weak and there were times when his physical ability to withstand more therapies became worrisome. He never questioned stopping treatment (if he did, he didn't share that with anyone).

He was so dedicated to providing for his family that he continued to work through some of the toughest treatment regimens while standing on his feet for hours at a stretch working as a chef. Never once did he complain.

114

I didn't have the opportunity to spend a lot of time with him individually but spent many hours with his family over the course of two years and because of them I got to know Jack.

In the medical world, we can become so committed to treating the illness that the person behind the disease can be lost. Jack was never lost; his family didn't let that happen. He spent the last two weeks of his life in the hospital. He and family knew he was dying and chose the hospital as his place of death.

Over the course of those weeks, as I was at bedside with Jack and his family, his personhood shined. They welcomed me into their lives as they shared stories of him. He was gracious and kind to everyone he met. While he had many career accomplishments, there was absolutely nothing that could compare to the pride he exuded when talking about his family. Nothing else was even a close second. During that time there were some really tough conversations, but one thing was clear. He needed his family to know he did everything imaginable to have just one more second with them.

They know.

They will hold on to his legacy as they navigate the world ahead without the heartbeat of their family. His son said it best, "He fought with a fierce and kind heart, the way we should all live our lives". Jack and his family are one of my reasons.

Anne Front

Her Eyes

Her body is frozen, but her eyes are full of story. Rhea sits in her wheelchair propped up, a neck guard to hold her head in place. Her wife, June, is attentive, intense, and glances back and forth from the computer screen to Rhea. The outpatient palliative care team members are in various Zoom squares, the new reality of telemedicine. Unlike meeting in person, faces are close, and our subtle shifts are easily observed. Rhea periodically drools or moans gutturally. June responds, quick and lovingly, with a towel or readjustment.

Rhea's Amyotrophic Lateral Sclerosis has progressed rapidly in the time our team has known her. Her eye-gaze machine allows her to write her thoughts, letter by letter, and then speak to us robotically. The pauses are long as we wait for Rhea to transcribe her words. June begins to chatter, filling up space, listing off recent concerns. Rhea's mechanical voice interrupts. She feels she is disappearing into a menu of only "yes" and "no". She lived a full life before her disease. A lawyer, a dynamo, with smooth

117

communication and an easy-going personality that opened many doors.

Now, Rhea feels voiceless and that she is fading away. She feels it among friends since it takes so long to communicate. And lately, more acutely with June as her care needs increase.

Staring into Rhea's eyes, brown and tearful, I feel her helplessness and despair. We sit in the heavy space of knowing and unknowing. It is not going to get better. Function by function, her abilities are disappearing. She is dying. I feel a seductive urge to skirt around the truth, to change the subject. But we are her team, and this moment requires honesty—whole-hearted presence and deep listening. Today, she has not died. She is alive, strong, and yearning to be heard. Her eyes challenge us. See me.

I breathe slowly, steadying myself. "Rhea, we see you. We hear you."

I validate feelings and lean into the palpable pain between them. Rhea, wanting to hold onto her personhood. June, wanting to hold onto Rhea, trying to manage needs with loving, sometimes overbearing, urgency.

"Yes, that's it. I want to tell her what I need instead of her guessing." Rhea replies.

I ask Rhea if she would be willing to endure some level of discomfort as the price of not getting her needs met immediately. I ask June if, when not an emergency, would June be willing to hold off on her knee-jerk reactions to hover?

"June doesn't want you to suffer. At the same time, Rhea, you want the chance to speak your mind fully." I pause as Rhea catches up.

Rhea's eyes light brighter. She feels heard. She shares that this would mean so much. After enduring so many challenges, she can tolerate pain until she can communicate fully what she needs to.

June's shoulders relax. She tells us about the burden of trying to mind-read, to anticipate and always react. She is tired. Their losses are stacking up. She misses the fullness of Rhea's voice and feels the changes in the relationship. She looks intensely into Rhea's eyes, connecting with the strong and capable person Rhea is. She agrees to try.

After the session, my eyes tear up. There is a gaping hole in the pit of my stomach. I feel empty and ineffective. I want to do more, to erase the pain that can't be wiped away. Rhea and June's losses are happening, and nothing will change that. My job is not to fix, but to bear witness to my patients, as people. Which ultimately starts with bearing witness to myself, as human.

I let the salty grief fill the hole in me, and eventually wash away. I take a deep in-breath and release out. I click the meeting invite for my next appointment, preparing for the eyes of my new patient.

Anne Kelemen

The Patient in Room 10

When we met, James was in his early thirties, dying in an intensive care unit (ICU) in the city hospital where I worked. Our palliative care team was asked to help with symptom management and transition to an inpatient hospice facility. Other members of the palliative care team had already met with him and suggested a social worker follow up because he had a history of trauma. Sitting at the bedside, in the cramped room of the ICU, he shared a little about how he was physically feeling—his continuous dialysis machine making its rhythmic noises between his slow breaths. The doctors told him that morning they didn't expect him to live longer than a week once dialysis stopped.

I was relatively new to palliative care social work, eager to explore his worries, I jumped in quickly, asked how he was coping, and was not prepared for what came next.

He said, "I'm scared."

Eager, again to help him process, I asked, "are you scared of the physical aspects of dying, or what comes next?"

121

He reflected, "what comes next because I have killed people."

My mind, like a tilt a whirl, tried quickly to funnel my racing thoughts; I felt helpless, nothing in social work school prepared me for this, I judged myself for asking that question. I froze, unable to think of anything comforting. The truth is, I too felt scared for him. Social work school had taught me stern boundaries, and while my instincts told me to reach out and hold his hand, I worried this would be too intimate. Would holding his hand cross some boundary between clinician and patient? As his tears continued to flow freely, I trusted my instincts and after a few seconds, looked up, focused on his teary eyes, took a few breaths, and reached nervously for his hand.

He went on to share that his father was killed by the police before his first birthday, his mother died of an overdose when he was ten. When he was in his early teens and involved in some criminal behavior, the court system tried him as an adult. He spent the next twenty something years in prison, being known as a number and not a name, and here he was in an ICU, often dehumanized in the same way and referred to as—"the patient in room 10" He trusted me with his story, his fears, and I saw another human desperate for answers, of which I had none, and realized it was okay not to have answers. So I remained silent and listened. So, James and I sat together, holding hands while he cried, and after some time, a shift in his body happened and he said, "thank you" and I took my cue to leave.

I didn't have a word for it that day but learned this clinical term recently from Dr. Tashel Bordere—suffocated grief. James' profound grief in those moments we spent together before he left for hospice, had long been suffocated. He spent most of his life within a system that did not allow him to grieve, for his father, his mother and for the people he killed. I have come to view his death, and many of the deaths I see in this work, as systemic killings. James was one of many, Black men who are quickly, or in James's case, slowly suffocated within a system of injustice, some who die within seconds on the streets. Others die after years of suffocation within the unjust healthcare system. So, for James and many others, I continue this work and I often forgo those rigid boundaries I learned in the classroom and lean into the human connection.

Charisse Knowlan

Being Present

I was a brand new social worker on a general medicine unit when asked to see a patient who wished to explore his thoughts and fears about dying and to discuss end-of-life options including curiosity about medically assisted death. I felt trepidation, overwhelm, and questioned whether I was prepared for this kind of conversation. Nevertheless, a referral was received, and I had to respond.

Nervously, I approached the patient, eager to do a good job but feeling totally out of my depth. What am I supposed to say about dying? What could I possibly have to offer in the face of this enormously significant moment in this person's life? My education had provided training, skills, and knowledge but I felt completely unprepared for the gravity of this kind of conversation.

As I introduced myself and my role, I was greeted warmly by a man in his 80s. He shared that he'd been living with a chronic, life-limiting disease for some time and acknowledged as he was getting older that things were getting harder to manage as disease progressed. He lamented the increased admissions to hospital and the shorter periods of time spent at home. He struggled with feeling less in control, less independent, and unable to do the enjoyable things that gave his life quality. He knew things were changing, fast, but wasn't quite sure what to do about it.

And so, without knowing quite what to offer this person or what he needed from me, I decided to be present. We spent over an hour together as he reviewed his life. He told me about his childhood, glory days, triumphs, and failures. He reflected on regrets, wondered what he might have done differently, and smiled as he remembered the cherished relationships. He was now mostly alone in the world, with family and close friends gone before him, but he held tightly to the deep connections he had with loved ones throughout life.

He talked about his values and how they'd changed as he grew and evolved as a person, and which values held strongly throughout. He talked about the purpose of his life and pondered whether there really needed to be a purpose at all. He shared thoughts on the meta-physical, what he believed happened when someone dies, and contemplated his spirituality, wrestling with what it meant at this point.

At the end of our conversation, he expressed feeling a deeper sense of knowing how his death might look, having reflected on who he was and what continued to be important. He was moved to another unit shortly after and while I don't know what the final chapter was like or how he died, I will always remember the importance, both for him and myself, of that time spent together reflecting, laughing, observing the hard moments, and remembering. I realized that despite my skills, training, and education, and despite my fears and self-doubt, my greatest offering in that moment was to be completely present to witness a significant moment in his life as he reflected and unpacked.

I have since begun working on an in-patient palliative care unit and am privileged to share beautiful, touching, painful, and life-changing experiences with patients and their families every day. It is not always easy, it is not always beautiful, reflective practice, but it is always meaningful and reminds me of the great difference that truly being present for someone else can make.

Lauren LaTourette

Sacred Space

I t was a Saturday, an unusual day to put on my helmet and cycle toward the hospital. I arrived ahead of Sarah's husband who was planning to bring in their two young children for the first visit: One who hadn't seen his mother in months; the other since birth. An anxious toddler cried on and off, confused and frightened at the sight and sounds of a ventilator, ECMO, and various alarms. A newborn slept soundly, snuggled in a relative's arms close to the bedside. Intimate moments, in which Sarah was able to spend wakeful time in the presence of her family, time that had been taken from her due to COVID. As a new life had begun in their family, another was trying to survive. Per request, I stood on the other side of a smartphone camera and took several family photos. I captured moments of the four of them all together while Sarah tearfully held her newborn's hand. This image is forever ingrained in my memory.

I hold on to the incredible resilience of Sarah's husband who managed it all through the darkest of days. For the nursing staff, who day in and day out showed up to give

127

impeccable care and for the providers and residents who gave their best through a long and complicated road.

Now a couple of years later, I sit at the bedside talking with Carmen, a woman in her forties, alone and grappling with a rapidly progressive cancer diagnosis. Just weeks ago, she was enjoying life with her young family without concern for her mortality. Her extended family, across the world and separated by systems which create barriers to uniting families in times of urgent need. No matter the day, the intensity of symptoms, or the heaviness of updates from the medical teams, she never hesitates to express gratitude.

Each interaction with her leaves me with appreciation and amazement at her vulnerability to talk about fears of dying and leaving behind young children. For her attitude of gratitude toward a broken healthcare system, a position I'm not sure I could muster if in her shoes. I've always felt passionate about bearing witness to the moments in our patients' lives which are often easier to avoid. Engaging in tough conversations, showing up for the patient and family who need support, and continually embracing these moments week after week. Whether behind the smartphone camera for family photos, sitting in the needed silence with a young dying patient, sharing with grieving families, or supporting our colleagues in distress, how do we continually step into these moments and preserve our ability to continue forward?

For me, this question continued to arise as a once new palliative care social worker and in the traumatic times of a global pandemic. Often, I struggled to stay afloat through challenging days. As the weeks and years passed, I have recognized the privileged position of witnessing our patients' stories as we stand beside them through one of life's most intimate journeys. To listen to the patient as the expert of their experience, and to meet them at whatever place they may be within the course of their serious illness. Learning to be attentive to my own parallel processing, and frequently seeking out and creating safe spaces in which I can share and process these experiences renews my energy each week and enables me to continue this work alongside my talented colleagues.

Eunju Lee

A Dutiful Son

J-J died this morning, finally still, with a slight sliver of a smile, his eyes closed. With his chemo baldness, he looked not unlike a young Buddha, except white in pallor, cold to the touch. After two endless days of wrestling against his own body, unable to sit, to lie down, or rest his head on the pillow even with repeated and continuous doses of Ativan. He had fidgeted and squirmed, tossed and thrashed in unremitting struggle against his body's betrayal.

We, in end-of-life work, have a name for this: terminal restlessness. Why it comes to some and not others, its etiology, and, tragically, its remedies are unclear. We can only speculate about this body in transition, writhing like a chrysalis to shed life's outer layer.

I had my own speculations about the reasons for his suffering, his total pain, based on my shared cultural identity with J-J and his family. J-J was a man just thirty years old whose life was only beginning to open, and the only child of older Korean immigrant parents. They had tried to conceive a child for eleven years through multiple, painful miscarriages before he, their first and last child, was born, J-

J's mother confided. He embodied their labor, their suffering, their history, and their future. Through him, his mother's decades of working as a seamstress and his father's repeated opening and then closing of businesses in failure, would have meaning. J-J was to be the remedy and healing from the strain and ruptures in his parents' marriage caused by decades of rising at dawn to squint at the needled thread of a sewing machine, the humiliation of shuttering businesses because financial capital without social and cultural capital is insufficient, and the unremitting debasement of everyday racism of being forever alien in their new land.

This was the Han (한, 恨) of J-J's parents; Han being a uniquely Korean concept that expresses a cultural identity of sorrow, regret, grief, resentment, and a dull ache of the soul, has no easy English translation. It is an identity borne out of the country's long history of invasions, oppression, and suffering, a form of internalized intergenerational trauma. In the swirl of this deep pain, cultural traditions and values serve as life's fulcrums. Foremost among them is filial piety.

According to the tenants of filial piety fundamental to the Confucianism of Korea, there is no greater transgression than a wayward disobedient child ignorant of the sacrifices of their parents. And there is nothing more treacherous, more impertinent, and dishonorable than the destruction of the body given to you by your ancestors. So sacred is this gift that even clipping fingernails and hair was done with reverence and care. Every strand of hair and fleck of skin belong to our parents as much as to ourselves.

Caring for our body then is the beginning of filial piety and death, the ultimate act of impertinence, even if it is not of your own choosing, even if it is because your body is riddled with cancer. So, I wondered, how was J-J to screech out his deep guilt, his culpability, his need for forgiveness from his parents other than to fight his own peace? How is a child able to convey the depth of their debt to their parents who not only gave life, but must also lay them in the ground? How is a child to absolve themself of their feckless, thoughtless life? A life that would abandon one's parents to perennially unsatiated grief?

So, J-J squirmed and twisted and railed against his own dying body. What else could he do to express his self-reproach, self-condemnation, and contrition but to deny his own body the rest it was seeking.

Jennifer Christophel Lichti

On Offering and Receiving Safe Spaces

I no longer remember his name, but I still feel the thread of connection formed in our one encounter, one afternoon, down the hall from his mother's hospital room. As the mother of a young child myself, I came prepared to meet my patient's child with an armful of books, art supplies and games. I remember entering that space with a keen awareness of how my own fears might be triggered in this interaction, then setting an intention to stay focused on this child's unique needs at this traumatic time of anticipated loss.

The child's father joined us initially, sharing a concern that his young son may have emotions that could be hard to describe in words. He asked the child's permission to leave us—reassuring him of our close proximity to his mother's room. As soon as the door closed, the child eagerly reached for the art supplies. I offered an activity commonly used in my past work at a child and family bereavement program.

"If I draw a big heart on this paper, would you like to put something inside?" He nodded, and immediately began to communicate with the crayons and markers.

The first heart rapidly filled with red, orange, and yellow. He drew with a fierce focus and intensity. When it was finished, he told the story of a train accident, fire, injuries, and emergency vehicles. I could feel the heat and the devastation—the trauma.

Without pause, he looked up with a sense of urgency and asked, "Can we do another?"

The drawings in the next heart were mostly green and blue. There was a patch of grass where he enjoyed walking with his mother on sunny days. Then the illustrations took a turn as the mother and child suddenly fell down a hole and became trapped in a "jail of ice." The child explained that it was dark in that space, and they could no longer see each other. I asked if they could still talk to one another through the walls, and he assured me that they could. I could feel the cold, sadness, and loss.

Almost simultaneously, I felt the peace that came with this release. His body relaxed and the intensity waned. But he wasn't quite finished. I watched his eyes catch the sparkle of beads, some with letters on them. He asked for another heart, and we got out the glue. The colors on this heart were predominantly pink and purple. We spelled things with the beads and markers—messages for his mother. This one was meant for display on the hospital room wall.

Soon after, his father came to collect him, and he turned

to hand me the first two hearts. "I want you to keep these."

I followed them down the hall to the nurse's station and watched them enter the room together. The palliative care physician was standing nearby and noticed as I stood dazed for a moment, pondering the depth of emotion that had just been expressed and witnessed.

The physician came to stand next to me and quietly asked, "How are you doing?" With her words of acknowledgement, I suddenly felt drained of all my energy.

"I think I just used up everything I had for today," I responded.

"I can see that in your face," she said, "that must have been a tough one."

This work is about giving and receiving. It's about caring for our patient and families and being a part of teams that demonstrate care for one another. Palliative care social workers often take the lead in nurturing team health, and we can get caught up in all of that noticing, listening, and giving.

When one of our teammates pauses to attend to our needs, and we are offered a chance to be seen and heard, it can bring balance and renewal in those moments when we sit in those spaces together.

Alba C. Lopez

The Intensive Care Unit in the Time of COVID

The early days of the COVID pandemic and quarantine was a time of uncertainty and fear everywhere. At the VA Hospital, as I am sure it was the same at many hospitals, the lobby was empty except for staff screening arriving employees. Outpatient clinics were closed, waiting rooms were empty and the corridors lacked traffic and the noises associated with a busy medical center.

The medical units that housed the earliest COVID patients were eerily quiet as staff socially distanced, masked and covered up. The patient rooms on the designated COVID units were adapted for ventilation directly out of the hospital and the doors to their rooms remained closed. The patients were isolated, receiving contact from individuals behind masks, face shields and gloves. There was no reassuring touch. Interactions were efficient, task oriented and often hurried. I often wondered if this is what it was like in the early days of the AIDS crisis where the combination of misinformation and the need for education caused panic. Many of those afflicted with HIV were shunned by some and the more marginalized members of that cohort were often isolated and faced their last hours alone.

The days of "team huddles", in-person reports and morning rounds were replaced by Webex and Teams meetings. The art of "healing touch" was now done through masks and from a "social distance." Notably absent at the bedside of the dying were the family members. The hospital was not permitting any visitors and only essential healthcare staff were permitted on site. Family meetings and goals of care discussions were now done by phone or computer meetings. The ICU beds were full and many of the individuals that arrived in the earliest days of the pandemic were the most compromised.

There was a patient in the ICU with a very poor prognosis, who did not have COVID but had experienced a stroke and had been placed on a ventilator. His family was unable to visit at a time that would have otherwise allowed them to be at his bedside, hold his hand and offer words of comfort and final goodbyes. This opportunity was abruptly stopped with the lock down. The desperation and anger expressed by the family was understandable. The compromise was to allow a staff member to enter the room with a tablet so the family could talk with the patient twice a day for a half hour. During the month that followed, I would hear the most heartfelt pleas for the loved one to "get up and get better" every day. It was a sacred space and at times I felt like a necessary intruder as the technology required human assistance so that the family could survey the patient's room, observe his care, and communicate with his team. Due to his medical state, the patient could not respond verbally. The ability to have the family present in this way was a measure of comfort provided to both patient and his family. Uncertain times required creative approaches. It was very humbling and touching.

In another room there was a young man who was succumbing to cirrhosis and COVID. He was able to speak with his mother and sister who offered words of love and support. The patient heard them and smiled. He told them he loved them and they saw his face a final time before he passed away later that evening.

I have been a social worker for over thirty years and have often held the hands of the dying and their family and friends. I believe that these two patients will stay with me as two of the most intimate in terms of shared space and the journey taken by the dying and their families. Technology can bridge gaps, caring comes in many forms and in times of uncertainty and isolation we find new strengths.

Ta'Tiana Miles

Is Informed Consent Really Informed Consent?!

I have not always been a palliative care social worker, much of my work in the hospital has been in case management. In fact, I always found myself trying to understand what it is and if there really was a need for another social worker in the room. You know, the silo effect. It was not until one of my assignments as a travel social worker with a palliative care team that I realized their value.

I met a young Black man named Dylan who was the same age as I was at the time twenty-eight. Vibrant and full of life, yet he was in the hospital with the need for palliative care. Dylan had diabetes that was complicated by kidney failure and was ultimately treated with a renal transplant. About thirty days post-op, Dylan developed some severe transplant complications including skin disruption, disfigurement, and severe uncontrolled pain. Our palliative care team was consulted to assist with pain management and psychosocial support.

I completed a chart review and immediately became concerned as I learned that the organ the patient received came from a donor who was hepatitis C and syphilis positive. I immediately began to question if the patient was aware that the donor was positive for these diseases and if he was aware, did he fully understand what that meant to receive an organ from a "high risk" donor. I also wondered, did this patient and his family receive all the correct information that was needed to make an informed decision, or did they just get passed off as another Black family that should be thankful to receive an organ? I was left with a pit in my stomach that I could not shake, ultimately feeling disheartened and anxious for my patient's wellbeing.

Dylan could not talk much secondary to his pain, but he did often try to smile to let others in the room know that he was "okay." He would attempt to even give a thumbs up at times. I remember meeting his mother and she talked about how her son was her best friend and shared all the hopes and dreams that he wanted to accomplish. I remember standing in the gaps to fill the space to provide support to this family who was ultimately losing their young son. There is something about watching a young person struggle at the end of their life and supporting the anticipatory grief of the family: That grief is unmatched. Dylan did die but his life changed my view of the work that palliative care social workers do.

Was this family truly provided informed consent? I

never got the answer to that. Would this organ have been offered to a patient without melanated skin? I am not sure. My questions still linger with me as does Dylan, his life, and his death. Now when I come across transplant patients and patients seeking treatment for any disease I wonder, how often do our patients experience an informed consent process that truly matters?

Abigail Nathanson

The Sadness, the Madness and God

My patient said to me, "I wish I were God", in a moment when her composed visage dropped, and she let me see some of her angst. I asked her why, what would be different if she were God?

"I wouldn't have to be scared anymore."

I could appreciate how much pain she had to be in, not just to need God, but where she had to *be* God to find relief. She had come to me a few months ago, ostensibly for grief counseling, but letting me know in no uncertain terms that she was not looking to be consoled.

"She refuses to be comforted for her children, because they are no more," was her oft-quoted line from the Bible.

A few months later, I offered her a similar one from Sigmund Freud I had come across in a letter he wrote after the death of his daughter: In it, he too wrote about being inconsolable, and how a loss can never be fully filled, and serves as a way to maintain connection to love.

It, too, resonated deeply for her, and she seemed grateful to be understood in that moment. She did not know what

142

she wanted, nor believe that anything could help; she just knew this was, unbearably, her worst nightmare.

I could work to hold space for as much of her horror as we could muster, and bear witness. I could help her digest and understand a little bit of it at a time, and I wondered whether that was enough. While she was remarkably resilient, I worried about how she was going to tolerate being in so much agony. In reflecting on my own countertransference, I ask myself: do I think I need to be God to help, too?

The words of three of my patients came to mind as I reflected on my work with her, and I tried to freely associate and allow them to pop into my head, without anticipating why:

"It's the sadness and the madness," as one person described her dual grief and caregiving.

"Maybe I don't have to be the answer to everyone's problems," said another person, gently learning how to find her voice.

"It's like 'pinning the tail' on 'what-the-fuck,'" described a third person, caught in the excruciating uncertainty of his father's illness.

As much as these words represented the wisdom they found in their own experiences, in another context, these words resonated for me and my work with this patient's uncertainties, too. There is some sadness and some madness in bearing witness to such despair, and continual lessons on not trying to make myself the answer to unanswerable questions. I will also heed the wisdom of my last patient and recognize the absurdity in trying to "pin the tail" on this work together.

And so, in the absence of a neat, definitive bow on her process or mine, I will try to just embrace the sadness, embrace the madness, and trust that 'what-the-fuck' will probably be okay without a tail for a while.

Carina Oltmann

The Rich Tapestry of Serious Illness Care

"In life there are 10,000 joys and 10,000 sorrows."

I have pondered this well-known Buddhist saying so often over the course of my career as a palliative social worker. It brings ease to my being and helps make meaning and sense of the suffering we witness.

Serious illness can cast a dark shadow across the landscape of life. Oftentimes we, and especially those living with serious illness, struggle to make sense of the randomness of disease. How can a young twenty-two-year-old have end-stage cancer? How can an older adult lie almost lifeless, connected to so many tubes without a say in their care? In what way can I best engage a spouse who is now preparing to support his children as they say goodbye to their mother, who is at end of life and receiving hospice care with a diagnosis of widely metastatic breast cancer?

There are no easy answers to these questions, but I have learned to find and make meaning in this work. "Zooming out," I can envision the larger tapestry of the person's life, including the lovely threads of joy, connection, love,

145

accomplishment, and success. These are, of course, interwoven with periods of sorrow, including loss, grief, suffering, and disconnect.

I sit with Anamaria, a lovely fifty-two-year-old woman with advanced pancreatic cancer. She is tearful as she talks about the death of her young daughter several years ago. As Anamaria faces her own mortality, she reflects on the profound grief she has experienced over the loss of her daughter. I hold space for her and her grief, I tear up as she shares in such a vulnerable and open way and invite her to explore the meaning she makes of such sorrow. Anamaria's face softens as she talks about her son, who is now studying to become a nurse after having cared for his sister and now his mother. She notes how proud she is of him and the simple joy of spending time with him. Anamaria talks about the crafting they do together and the peace she feels when she is beside him, creating miniature-stained glass pieces to hang in the window. Within this narrative I gauge the deep joy she has felt in motherhood even in the face of losing her daughter.

Sitting with clients and patients with serious illness is profoundly meaningful as we take part in alleviating physical, emotional and existential distress. Supporting the journey of our clients, patients, and families as they build the narrative of their illness and of life in general is deeply gratifying work. To be instrumental in weaving together the threads of joy with the threads of sorrow, then stepping back and beholding the tapestry of their life is a privilege, one that I will cherish as one of my own great joys in life.

Nick Purol

When I'm Gone

I met "Nash", an eighteen-year-old young man with metastatic cancer, as part of a palliative care consultation. He told me that he was currently a medical student at this very teaching hospital, working on pivotal cancer research that would lead to a cure, planning to finish an upcoming marathon despite having never run before, and going to propose to one of his nurses. None of these things were accurate or possible—but they were true to him. Within days of meeting Nash, he told me with neither guile nor irony, "you'll be so sad when I'm gone. I'm so sorry that I have to leave you."

When I remember Nash, I think about how pediatric palliative care is often absurd. Children aren't supposed to die, they aren't supposed to get seriously ill. When they do, they are supposed to be adorably bald, noble heroes who endure and then get better. None of our pediatric systems are built to accommodate a seriously ill young person with underlying mental health challenges and limited supports. Yet, in reality, many adults with their long list of comorbidities are cared for in pediatric centers, where the liminal space between "child" and "adult" extends indefinitely. There are no perfect patients, just imperfect systems.

While sometimes loved and charming to staff, Nash had a reputation for being "challenging" due to his self-advocacy, often unrealistic expectations of clinician time, and anger when confronted with challenges to his truths. He loved to talk about his impending death: how he would be buried (in a lavish ceremony), honored (with great praise and posthumous Ivy League honorary degrees), and remembered (as an inspiration, hero, scholar). He discussed his own long psychiatric history, confusion in social situations, and how it worried him. He distanced himself from his working-class Chinese American immigrant parents, who did everything in their ability to support, love, and accept him. He stated that he, unlike them, was Christian, highly educated, and "westernized." He would talk frankly about the importance of only going to an elite institution, marrying a white woman, and amassing wealth, accolades, and recognition.

When I remember Nash, I think about how he could succinctly and disturbingly highlight how our underlying cultural structures are shaped by hierarchies, racism, and class. It seemed he felt he could be loved only if he looked like most of his providers, assimilated fully, and rejected his familial traditions in favor of embracing a wealthy, white, and highly educated framework. Through his assumptions of how to accumulate prestige and respect, he reflected something deep and uncomfortable in the world about who and what holds power, praise, and importance. When I remember Nash, I reflect on my own privilege as a white, cisgendered man and my participation in fraught systems of power—even when seeking to do good.

"I am going to die today," Nash confidently told me. He often held an unattached oxygen mask to his face, despite not being particularly air-hungry. "You're going to be so sad without me." He would then take off his mask, close his eyes, and wait. It would take many more weeks before his breathing was truly impacted from his spreading disease, and until then, "I am going to die today" became an oddly ritualized way to say goodbye.

When I remember Nash, I *think* I know he was telling me how he hoped he would be remembered, how lonely he was, the importance of even the most fleeting of connections, and the unending search for acceptance and respect. I remember the halo of distress that followed him from unit to unit, to a hospice house, and back to the hospital in his final days. I remember the often painful, accidental truths he shared in casual conversation. I remember his pride and his genuine desire to delineate his accomplishments and his impact on the world. I think what I remember most, however, is how correct he was. Despite the self-awareness that supposedly comes with our profession, I do miss Nash deeply, uniquely. I am sad I didn't get to see more, to understand better. I hope that is a small way to honor him.

Maxxine Rattner

Stay

To this day, I remember the agony, the deep wailing bellows flowing out of her—a young girl, eleven or twelve years old—after her mother's death. She had arrived, after school, to visit with her mom at hospice. I don't quite recall if her mom had just died, somewhat unexpectedly before she arrived (yes, many deaths in hospice are painfully unexpected), or whether it was shortly after she had said hello and then stepped out of her mom's room, likely visiting the hospice kitchen for a freshly baked snack. But I remember having to share the news with her. And I remember the sounds and words that emanated out of her as she heard, took in, and integrated this news into her being.

"Mommy, please don't go!! Mommy I need you!!!"

I remember my colleagues' faces as they looked at me, wide eyed, and slowly backed out of the room, leaving me to hold this space, to hold this immense grief…

I remember feeling wholly unsure how to do this.

How to hold space for and support this expression of intense pain, intense grief, intense suffering.

152

"Can I be here beside you?" I asked.

I remember her nodding as she wailed.

"I'm right here with you."

I remember trying, too, to hold space for a family friend who was also in the room. I remember they looked at me imploringly, as if to say, how do I help her? I tried to support them in supporting her; to reassure them that this is exactly how it needed to be, and there was nothing to change or do, other than to sit close and ride her waves of anguish alongside her. I would need to remind them of this several times as the minutes (was it hours?) wore on.

A hospice volunteer would tell me months later that they had never heard sounds throughout the hospice like the ones they heard that evening—sounds I didn't quiet, or question.

After some time,

I'm not sure when,

the sounds became more quiet, muffled.

Alongside—or with—the intense pain, grief and suffering, was immense inner knowing.

She peeled pictures of her and her mother off the room walls and placed them around her mom. She put a side ponytail in her mom's long hair. She knew what she needed. And that was what she did.

Stacy S. Remke

Home Care: A Practice Reflection

We received the referral as a sort of last ditch request. "We know it won't work out but it's her last wish so we have to try," said her doctor.

She was seventeen, had been in the hospital for months, diagnosed with her third relapse of colon cancer. It was a rare condition for someone her age. She had defied many odds, not least of which was her family circumstances, which I am still not sure about. She had the most chaotic back story I ever heard, before or since. We didn't really know who her parents were, or who had raised her to this point. She had essentially been parenting herself for years already. But there was an identified "dad" who wanted to care for her, and grandparents she had only met a couple of months before, who had said she could come to live with them and they would take care of her.

Of course, we would give it a try. We met her family, formulated a plan, and got organized. The first home visit was a challenge. Her grandparents were crafters and hobbyists, which is maybe a nice way of saying hoarders.

The house was stuffed with materials of all sorts. There was a narrow path through the living room to the bedrooms. She had a ferret that roved through the house's passageways, tumbling in a violet lucite ball. The nurses and I took deep breaths and proceeded. We worked around things as they were. We grew to enjoy her family and all their quirks, respecting their devotion to her, their care in spite of their limited means and no clue about what they were getting into. They were patient, responsive, and vigilant. They were pretty concrete about things, and that served them well in this situation. They focused on what they had to and didn't speculate or project into the future much.

Over the next few months she kept active. She went to church youth group, took a Make-a-Wish trip—a cruise to Alaska with this new family of hers, and went out dancing with her infusion pump tucked inside her shoulder bag. As her condition declined, she had palliative radiation. She said the burns she got as a result were the worst pain of all her treatments. She became more fatigued and stayed home more. I think she was relaxing into this family care that allowed her to experience a safe home for the first time.

One day, she was excited to tell me about a big dream she had. She saw Heaven in her dream, and felt it was a vision of her future. Her dream removed all fears about dying. She was so happy, beaming as she related the dream to me. I was glad to be able to affirm the power and truth of dreams, wherever they come from.

A few days later, she was crying and anxious. She had told her youth pastor about her dream. He had denounced it as the work of the devil. She was absolutely crushed. This pastor and the youth group were among her main sources of support. Our chaplain was able to counsel her about the dream, validating her experience while also helping her find a way back into the fold of the youth group.

She continued to decline, became homebound, and then confined to bed, her world becoming smaller. Yet she managed that with grace and humor. Death came peacefully, with one of her steadfast nurses at her side. Her grandmother wept softly at her bedside, then wiped away tears as she got back to business as was her way.

I am so glad I got to know this girl, and witness the coming together of friends, her chosen family and professionals to help her experience the love and care of home. I will also always remember what I learned from her: We can work with what is and trust the integrity of each person's path. Dying takes care of itself.

Rachel Rusch

The Story

"Good luck in there."
"He's difficult to work with."
"Non-compliant."

Familiar are these patient descriptors when working in palliative care. Our well-caring colleagues caught complicit within a system that brings such conclusions forward. A system too fast, too understaffed, too entrenched in systemic and historic oppression of marginalized communities. A system that allows the 'non-compliant' to be forever existing on the outskirts of our care. "I don't think he 'gets it.'" "We don't know what else to do."

I met Noel alongside my team with these words buzzing around us as we sanitized our hands, donned our gowns, fit our hands into gloves and covered our faces with masks. The mix of urgency and surrender palpable. The need to put these words gently aside communicated with quick looks exchanged as we knocked on Noel's door.

Entering Noel's room, we were met by a young man sitting comfortably crossed-legged in his bed—surrounded by books and tools that signaled an interest in the creative. His eyes ablaze with a mix of light and fear and wonder, he turned down his music as he'd undoubtedly been conditioned to do after years of living within a hospital system.

We sat down and introduced ourselves—our standard introduction where we aim to say that we are here to learn about Noel's story, to see how we may be an extra layer of support.

"I dunno. Can't they tell you about me?" Noel asked—gesturing to the door where the whispers of non-compliant, difficult, depressed were waiting to scratch their way in.

What proceeded was a long visit filled with silence. A silence led and comfortably held by Noel. This holding space became of his creation, perhaps seeing what this team truly meant by learning about his lived experience. An experience of quiet alertness, constant beeping, soft music and nurses entering at regular intervals to remind Noel to take his afternoon meds. Could we stay in this space with him? Could we really tolerate the smallest peak into his world?

We exited Noel's room with an invitation to return.

"You were in there for so long. What solutions do you recommend?"

We shared that we learned that Noel loves movies and

158

painting, that he's studying to be an artist. We shared that he didn't want to talk about his illness quite yet. We shared that it was clear that his team cared for him—and that this care felt hard right now.

"You were in there for so long."

Upon our next visit, the buzzing outside Noel's door as we readied to enter became louder. The system felt like it was taking shape into a Being with taloned hands and raised hackles. One that could grip our hearts and our intentions too.

"Oh hello" Noel said, inviting us into his quiet holding space. Some time passed.

"It's just hard for me to talk sometimes."

We paused. We noticed a well-worn notebook by his bed. We asked if it would be easier for him to write his thoughts down. He swiftly took up her notebook. He began to write.

What continued was Noel's story. A story of Noel's gigantic and powerful dreams. A story of frustration for living with a serious illness. Noel's awareness that his dreams may never come to pass.

"How would you feel if you had dreams that you knew you may never achieve?" He wrote of living as a Black man within a medical system that he did not always trust. That he knew did not always trust him. He detailed an exquisite understanding of his disease. He wished others knew how difficult it all was. He wanted to live a life full of his aspirations—not a life full of hospital stays.

With permission, we shared this story with the waiting Being outside Noel's door. I wish I could say that the Being heard Noel's story and shape-shifted into a form that offered reprieve, remorse and a solution. Instead, there was a glimmer. A bright, discernable glimmer of possibility that something else might get through. That the stories of our patients, our well-caring colleagues, and our ability to listen, might be the start of the dismantling and rebuilding that we so desperately need.

S. "Eryl" Shermak

Feeling My Way into the Relational Heart of Practice

I went through the pandemic on the frontlines of community care social work practice in a small coastal city. It was still people's households where I went whenever feasible and telephone-only visits were a last resort. Being in the homes of clients was service as always, but not quite as before—conversations might happen on a drafty porch, in a rain-soaked backyard, or once a reclaimed goat shed. Just as before, myself, families, and care recipients navigated the borderlands one finds between living and dying. Yet, unlike before, we were doing our best to mediate the new gradients of unknowing in the world at large.

As a practitioner, I thought often of the artist Emily Carr who was known for her dedicated practice of experimenting with how to translate the world as she saw it onto paper— unsure as she went along yet getting closer all the while to an outcome she knew to be authentic and vibrant. With her usual candor, Emily once said that one would have to try things out for themselves and that it was perfectly alright to not be sure of what one was doing, as you were feeling your way into it.

In an odd twist of fate, just as the pandemic was winding down and as I was now well-situated in dynamic routines, I was offered a newly formed social work role—one that a growing number of people would say offered a most welcome form of practice; virtual-only service. I was hesitant to return to the embodied experience of not quite knowing what I was doing. Yet at the same time, the palliative and pandemic practitioner parts of me recognized the value of my past experiments with finding my way and how this was yet another encounter with uncertainty and complexity. So, I became a virtual-only practitioner whose primary focus was to support family caregivers who were navigating challenging illness experiences, including around the end of life. In so doing, I would apply my palliative care experience and skills in novel ways. My role would include providing one-on-one counselling sessions, a series of skill-building workshops, and eventually group counselling. All offered through virtual and electronic means.

How would I work relationally with clients in their homes, but in a virtual way? Again, I returned to thinking about Emily Carr who had gone from creating landscape studies that solely depicted the world like a photograph, to ones considered to be highly abstract while being vividly accurate in how they illuminated the heart and energy of a place. As I found my way into the virtual role, a modality I had once seen as a less collaborative and dynamic practice, I kept close in mind the relational heart of a palliative approach. I strove anew for seeking and embracing the nuances of human connection between myself and those I supported; leaning into the emotions cast by facial expressions as seen across a Zoom link and becoming highly attuned to the stories that different tones of voice had to tell over the screen. In other words, I kept getting closer to an outcome for client care I knew to be deeply client-centered—one that is authentic and vibrant.

EPILOGUES

The epilogues that follow, without intent and plan, capture one of the most essential challenges in our work and our lives ...to bridge, honor the lens and lived experiences beyond ourselves. Simply reading the perspectives and intentions surrounding a symbolic and multilayered decision —capitalize or not—Black and White—invites us to join the dialogue and envision what we might create should we even begin to imagine and respect the lens through which we uniquely view the world.

Terry Altilio

Over decades of practice I have had rich opportunity to practice, teach, write, collaborate and think with colleagues across professions. I have been touched and enriched by the lives of perhaps thousands of patients and their families. Working on the first and second editions of the Oxford Text of Palliative Social Work and Palliative Care: A Guide for Health Social Workers has been memorable in many respects. Yet I carried a lingering and nagging thought. "*I have one book left in me.*" That book was simply a compilation of reflections, stories of experiences that inform our legacies and in a parallel way honor the legacies of patients, families, and colleagues, both affirming and broadening the lens through which we view our work and our lives. This is that book—a compilation written by a cadre of social workers who have shared stories that may touch readers no matter their profession or relationship to serious illness.

The process of sharing in the creation of this "*one book left in me*" with Anne, Arika and Vickie has been a most "autonomous" process as Vickie and Anne led us into the world of "self-publishing." The collaborations with editors and authors has deepened relationships and required that we discover and relate to how unique experiences influence how we work, learn and see the world. As we read reflections, attention to patient and family confidentiality led us to a thoughtfulness about team and institutional confidentiality. Attention to word choice and labels led to shared learning and discussion—not always unanimity - about decisions most poignantly represented by differing views as to whether one capitalizes both Black and White when referring to persons.

This process of reading, editing, re-reading and negotiating with each other and with authors has distilled a volume that reflects a sampling of the depth of our work, each written by unique voices and styles of writing. Authors have provided a lens that captures a range of experiences, sometimes bridging distance and separateness, sometimes sharing the suffering that comes when we observe and participate in care that oppresses and separates.

It was not possible to include all who have stories to share. This is a sampling of reflections brought to a published page to validate the legacy you all carry and continue to create in the care and compassion given and received.

Anne Kelemen

This book grew from conversations about stories and legacy and not just the stories we share when things go well, or how much it's an "honor" and "privilege" to do this work. The stories we carry that sometimes are too painful to share, the ones we as clinicians struggle to find meaning, where we witness intense suffering and realize it's not the death that is hard but the struggle before death that is a large part of the work in serious illness care. I am grateful for Arika, Terry and Vickie and their willingness to engage in this work and bring this book to life.

In editing this book, it was my hope that it would bring the readers some sense of peace and community. This book is about reflections honoring patients and their families where others have dealt with the death of a colleague, or death of a parent. Both something I have experienced, and this shared community provided me with healing I didn't know I needed too.

My father died twenty years ago, and as I finish this epilogue, I feel a lot of grief and sadness that he won't be here to read this, and I also know I would not have found this profession without his death. When my father was a child, he created a newspaper called *True News* that he and his friends sold in the neighborhood for a nickel. It was about neighborhood gossip and their window into the truth of what was happening in the early 1960s in their small town. I like to think this book is a small window into the *True News* of hospice and palliative care.

Vickie Leff

I'm very grateful for Terry Altilio having "one more book left in me" and being asked to join this incredible editing team. The process has been a pleasure and taught me a lot. Reading the profound, vulnerable and insightful reflections from our contributors has been an honor. We are so fortunate for these brave individuals who agreed to share what is in their heart. Social workers in palliative and hospice care have been telling these stories to each other, and colleagues, for many years. Real stories, real words and real consequences. It is comforting and affirming, knowing that we have shared experiences in this unique profession. We lean on each other, learn from each other and support each other. Thank you Terry, Anne and Arika.

My hope is this book will do the same for you. Whether you are a social worker, doctor, nurse, chaplain, child life therapist...we share a community in serious illness care. Being honest with ourselves and colleagues improves our practice, gives us hope and helps us do this work.

Arika Moore Patneaude

When asked to be a co-editor on *Mirrors and Windows: Reflections on the Journey in Serious Illness Practice*, there wasn't yet a title, or a clear path of what exactly the book was going to be about other than reflections by social workers. I had a sense though that it was going to be something important and personally impactful for me.

There were already three established editors, Anne, Vickie and Terry who had worked together before and seemingly knew each other quite well. I came into the group having only worked with Anne, though I had met Terry and knew who Vickie was. I was the only person of color, the only Black person and I entered into the space cautiously even though this experience is one that is lifelong and has been *lived* repeatedly. As our group began working together the well-studied group dynamics played out as it always seems to, no matter how small or large the size of the group. There were times we struggled with editorial decisions, some that were less important to me and others that were so hugely important to me that at times I wondered if it might be easier if I just left the group.

At times, remaining engaged in dialogue around some of these decisions, "*do we capitalize Black and white or do we not capitalize Black and white* ?" where I felt incredibly invested, pushed me way outside of my comfort zone. It was through individual conversation and understanding, frustration and tears, joy and laughter and growing trust *because* we, because *I* remained engaged, that this book has been shepherded to fruition. As each reflection came in, some in which I saw my own lived experience reflected as either a social worker or as a family member and others in which I learned something about the vulnerability and humility of my co-editors and my colleagues, something shifted for me.

I am deeply grateful to Anne, Vickie and Terry and each and every author, all who have shared the joy, frustration, hardship, heartbreak and gratitude of what it means to be a human caring for other humans in serious illness.

34416284R00106